CONTENTS

Maureen Keane, M.S., and Daniella Chace, M.S.
Foreword by John A. Lung, M.D.

WHAT TO EAT IF YOU HAVE CANCER

(UPDATED SECOND EDITION)

HEALING FOODS THAT BOOST YOUR IMMUNE SYSTEM

New York Chicago San Francisco Lisbon London Madrid Mexico City
Milan New Delhi San Juan Seoul Singapore Sydney Toronto

Library of Congress Cataloging-in-Publication Data

Keane, Maureen, 1950-
    What to eat if you have cancer : healing foods that boost your immune system /
Maureen Keane and Daniella Chace.
        p.   cm.
    Includes bibliographical references and index.
    ISBN 0-07-147396-3
      1. Cancer—Diet therapy.   2. Cancer—Nutritional aspects.   I. Chace,
Daniella.   II. Title.

RC271.D52K435   2007
616.99'40654—dc22   2006022555

*This book is dedicated to the memory of Michael J. O'Malley,
who died unexpectedly on Valentine's Day, 1996. A gentle giant of an
Irishman, Mike was known for his generous heart and willing hands.
His death has left a hole in all of us who loved him.*

1 2 3 4 5 6 7 8 9 0   FGR/FGR   0 9 8 7 6

ISBN-13: 978-0-07-147396-5
ISBN-10:   0-07-147396-3

McGraw-Hill books are available at special quantity discounts to use as premiums and sales promotions, or for use in corporate training programs. For more information, please write to the Director of Special Sales, Professional Publishing, McGraw-Hill, Two Penn Plaza, New York, NY 10121-2298. Or contact your local bookstore.

This book is printed on acid-free paper.

FOREWORD

The complex problems related to cancer continue to confound physicians and scientists, and, with the exception of lung cancer, the etiology of most malignancies is unknown. We have, however, discovered useful clues regarding the causes of cancer from population studies and epidemiological research. For example, developing countries do not suffer the cancer rates of modern society. The American cancer epidemic is linked to air and water pollution, food-chain contamination, food-processing techniques, smoking, drugs, constant stress (distress), obesity, and a sedentary lifestyle. All of these factors may be connected to cancer causation through nutritional imbalance. It is a recognized fact that two out of three women with breast cancer are obese. Nutritional status is affected by lifestyle choices and dietary habits. Our nutritional status either weakens us, promoting the development of cancer, or strengthens our bodies' defense mechanisms, enhancing our ability to prevent and/or control neoplastic processes.

Epidemiological studies and research into dietary habits suggest that specific, naturally occurring chemicals offer protection against cancer. Science has advanced in the realm of nutrition to a point where we can treat physiological imbalances with specific foods and related substances. For example, food components (antioxidants) may aid and strengthen the immune mechanism, and elements such as fiber may protect against the development of cancer. This publication may enlighten the cancer patient with information that is of extreme value in understanding the cancer process and its treatment. During the last twenty-five years, many patients under my care have questioned what they can do to change their lifestyles and enhance their ability to prevent and/or cure their malignancy. The information provided herein may prove extremely valuable in answering these queries.

These dietary protocols are suitable for patients at any stage of treatment. A change in lifestyle, including improved nutrition, may enhance traditional cancer therapy. This book defines a program of nutrition as an adjunct to medical cancer therapy. Improved dietary habits and an altered lifestyle may provide powerful support to conventional cancer treatments and, ultimately, the healing process. In the past, many cancer victims have found themselves involved in programs that do not approach the problem in a global, comprehensive manner. Those individuals who take an active, positive role in their treatment may enhance their chance of recovery and a complete cure.

—JOHN A. LUNG, M.D., CANCER SURGEON
MOUNTAIN STATES TUMOR INSTITUTE, BOISE, IDAHO

ACKNOWLEDGMENTS

For this second edition, Maureen wishes to thank her husband, John, for the love and support he gave through her cancer treatment, surgery, and recovery; her son, Micheál, for his computer expertise; and her feline accomplice, Maeve, for her constant companionship and unsolicited advice.

Both Daniella and Maureen want to thank their teachers at Bastyr University for sharing knowledge with them, Dr. John Lung for agreeing to write the Foreword with them, and David Stevenson for his illustrations.

INTRODUCTION

If you have been diagnosed with cancer, you remember with crystal clarity the moment you got the news. I will never forget.

It all started seventeen years ago on what appeared to be just another day. I was four months pregnant with my second child, and bending over was already difficult. Somehow I was sure this one was going to be a girl. My rough-and-tumble son was eighteen months old, and I was ready for a change. Toddler in tow, I had taken to window-shopping for baby clothes.

That day I bent to get a saucepan out of the lower cupboard. Cramps shot through my back, and as I stopped to catch my breath, I could feel the flow of warm blood. Two weeks and two ultrasounds later, we knew the baby had died. But the placenta hadn't; it was still alive and growing. Ten days after the D and C to remove the placenta and fetal remains, my gynecologist phoned. He wanted to see my husband and me in his office immediately. When I asked what was wrong, he simply said he had to discuss the pathology report on the D and C, and it was difficult to discuss "this type of thing" over the phone. I croaked out, "This isn't cancer, is it?" Pause. I've always hated pauses. "No, it isn't cancer." I could almost see him searching for the right words. "But it is something that can become cancer if it persists. But the D and C probably removed all of it."

A year later I was in an oncologist's office at the University of Washington. That something had apparently persisted. The placental cells of my dead baby were wandering my body, looking for a new home. But no need to worry, I was assured, they probably had spread only into the uterine wall. Chemotherapy should work; it almost always did.

After a CAT scan showed my lungs were clear, I began my first course of chemo with methotrexate. As I tried to get my mind off the needle the nurse was trying without success to stick into the back of my hand, I asked her, "If this disease spreads like cancer and it's treated like cancer, what makes it different from cancer?" She looked up into my eyes and then down again to work on my vein. "When it spreads like this," she said to my hand, "it is cancer." "Oh" was my only reply.

Somehow my first emotion was one of embarrassment. How could I have cancer and not know it? Why hadn't anyone bothered to tell me? *Of course, dummy*, I told myself, *you are seeing an oncologist in an oncology clinic being treated with chemotherapy by an oncology nurse. What did you think you had? But not cancer, not me.* I don't know what was worse those first few weeks: the side effects of the methotrexate or the knowledge that I had cancer. The C word. Not me.

Many friends gave me advice; others sent relics, medals, and cards. Everyone was praying. I made a point of going to a luncheon sponsored by the Irish club immediately after the first treatment. I wanted to show my friends that this disease was not going to get me down. It was the start of Irish week, and the committee in charge of the meal served corned beef and fresh horseradish with an Irish coffee chaser. No one had mentioned nutrition.

The first course of methotrexate didn't work. Neither did the second. "No problem," the doctor said. "The actinomycin will probably work." But the first course of actinomycin didn't work, and then neither did the second. My oncologist, Dr. Tamimi, was a great communicator. "You have three options," he told my husband and me over the phone. "Do nothing, and I guarantee you'll be dead in a year. We can put you in the hospital in the fall for combination chemotherapy that will make you quite ill. Or you can have surgery." We opted for surgery. I started one last course of chemo and then had my uterus and tubes removed.

That was twenty-seven years ago. My hair grew back and over time my scar even faded, but parts of my body never recovered. Within three years I had developed a chronic pain syndrome and migraines that eventually forced me to abandon my Irish dance school. The shortness of breath got a little worse every year until, sixteen years after my chemotherapy, I found myself back at the University of Washington, this time at their Pulmonary Hypertension Clinic being evaluated for a lung transplant. I avoided the transplant, but an intravenous drug kept me alive for six years. I had to have one drop every minute to keep my pulmonary arteries dilated enough for blood to get through my lungs.

Never once during those original sixteen months of tests and cancer treatment did any of my doctors, nurses, or other health care workers mention nutrition. I am convinced that if I had known then what I know now, a better diet and supplements could have protected the lining of my pulmonary arteries and prevented the damage.

The hospital back then took the "baby and the bathwater" approach to nutrition and cancer. If nutrition could not cure cancer, then nutrition was useless against cancer. Out the window they would toss it all. They did not understand the true nature of nutrition, which is one of help and support. Nutritional therapy helps your immune system to perform its job better while it supports your healthy cells and protects your body during the stress of cancer treatment.

Therefore, following the advice in this book will not, by itself, cure you of cancer. Nutrition therapy alone will not cure cancer no matter what some Internet sites claim. But when nutrition therapy is added to your traditional cancer treatment plan, it can increase your chance of cure as well as the quality of your life. Do your health care team a favor and join them. Together you have a much better chance at succeeding.

This book is divided into two parts. Part I is a primer on the body, cancer, and nutrition. It will introduce you to the vocabulary of cancer. Please take the time to read it. It will help you communicate with your doctor and make more informed decisions regarding nutrition. As much as we hate to say it, you will soon be a target for food supplement salespeople, many of whom will be very aggressive and very uneducated about nutrition and cancer.

Part II begins with a chapter on the various nutritional side effects associated with cancer treatment—highlighting particular problems, explaining what causes them, and suggesting solutions and strategies for coping. It also contains two diet plans with different menus designed to provide a high level of nutrition at various calorie levels. You'll also find meal planning for various conditions often experienced by cancer patients, from weight loss to coping with radiation therapy.

To develop your own personalized nutrition program, choose a diet and then add the recommendations for any side effects you may be experiencing. In the back of the book you will find references to help you participate in your treatment plan. These include a list of resources for information, support, and products, as well as details about products mentioned in the book.

Just a few words of caution: do *not* take large doses of any vitamin, food supplement, or herb without the knowledge of your oncologist. Some of them can negate the effects of some treatments.

This is the book I wish I'd had when I was first diagnosed. Daniella and I sincerely hope it helps you.

—MAUREEN KEANE

PART I

THE BODY, CANCER, AND NUTRITION

Getting diagnosed with cancer is somewhat similar to taking a crash course in medical school. Within a few months of your diagnosis you will know more about your particular cancer, the organ it is growing in, and the research being conducted than your original family doctor does. This self-education is vitally important to your recovery because knowledge is power—power over your disease and power over your treatment. Go to the library and read everything you can find on your particular situation. Start with your local library and work up to the medical library at the closest medical school. Get on the Internet and search the Internet for treatment options and patient discussion groups. Pick up the phone and call knowledgeable friends for information and advice. Join a support group, subscribe to newsletters, and keep reading and questioning. The more you know, the more options you will have.

Part I of this book was written to help you understand the concepts behind the words and terminology you will soon be learning. If you have just been diagnosed and know little about biology and cancer, this is the best place to start your education. These chapters simplify the anatomy of the body, the physiology of cancer, and the chemistry of nutrition. They explain how and why nutrition therapy works. This section is also a good introduction to nutrition and cancer treatment for spouses, family members, caregivers, and health care professionals. It will help them to understand what you are trying to accomplish.

1

The Microscopic World Inside You

To understand what cancer is and how it is treated, you must first become familiar with the miniature world of the cell. This is perhaps the most important chapter of the book, for the cellular level is where cancer begins and where nutrition exerts its effect. This chapter will help you understand the workings of the bodies of your cell citizens and how they divide when healthy.

Imagine for a minute that your body is a country and its cells are the citizens of your country. You, the president, live in the capitol building, the head. For a nation to be strong and healthy, its citizens must have honest work, proper tools to perform that work, a communication system, a transportation system, food and water, and a method to remove waste and trash. They must be protected from the environment and from attack by enemies from both within and without. With your help, the body is able to provide all of these necessities.

Your cell citizens come in all shapes, sizes, and abilities, and they perform an almost endless variety of jobs. Some

inhabit the great cities that are your organs; others prefer
to live in the country as far away from the bright lights as
possible—in your big toe, for instance. But no matter
where it lives, each cell has a purpose, an important job
that it performs for the good of that great nation, your
body: the United States of John or Jane Doe.

Basic Structure of a Cell

We begin this book with an examination of the average
cell citizen. When we were children, we were taught that
a cell was little more than a bag of water with a nucleus
floating inside. We fancied that a cell must resemble a raw
egg without the brittle outer shell and marveled we didn't
scramble ourselves.

Today we know that cells are highly structured. The
entire cell is filled with a cellular skeleton (or cytoskeleton), a three-dimensional scaffolding in which structures
called **organelles** are embedded. Organelles are like tiny
versions of your body's organs. Each of them has a specific
function, and when these functions are interfered with,
the result can affect the entire cell body. As science learns
more about how these structures work, some have become
targets for cancer treatments.

Each cell has a "skin" called the **plasma membrane**.
Attached to the outer surface of the plasma membrane are
many protein molecules. Some of these molecules lie on
top of the skin or membrane and serve as name tags, iden-
tifying to the outside environment what type of cell it is.
Other molecules, known as **receptor sites**, function as

attachment spots for hormones and other molecules, including the antibodies that are part of the immune system. Some molecules are found in groups of two or four and penetrate all the way through the surface of the membrane. These molecules act as a guarded door, allowing water and other small molecules to enter the cell. A single cell has thousands of these receptors, doors, and name tags on its surface.

To the naked eye, the largest and most obvious structure in the cell is its **nucleus**, which serves as a cellular brain. This round body is enclosed in a plasma membrane just like the skin that surrounds the cell. It holds the DNA that contains the encoded instructions for all cellular functions. All cells in the body, with the exception of the red blood cells, have at least one nucleus.

At the very core of the cell lies the **centrosome**, or microtubular organizing center. Extending from the centrosome is an impressive starburst of microtubules that reach outward toward the cell membrane. These hollow tubes and other cell filaments form the three-dimensional cytoskeleton that gives each cell its structure and form. Microtubules are composed of dumbbell-shaped molecules called tubulin dimers, which form a long chain that winds around a hollow core. Dimers add themselves to the bottom of the microtubules inside the centrosome so that the starburst grows outward. Dimers also take themselves off the other end, so that the microtubules are constantly assembling and disassembling. The average microtubule has a life of only ten minutes before it is disassembled into its dimers, which are then used to make another tubule. Microtubules are also the railroad tracks of the cell. Tubular motors travel outward along the microtubules carrying and dragging organelles and transport vesicles (see below) with them.

The outer membrane of the cell and the membrane of the nucleus are connected by means of a network of membrane-lined canals and sacs called the **endomembrane system**. This system acts as a transportation tunnel for protein products. Protein production actually begins in the nucleus when a portion of the DNA blueprint is copied onto messenger RNA (mRNA). If the protein is for export, the mRNA enters the start of the endomembrane tunnel, an organelle called the **endoplasmic reticulum (ER)**. Here the mRNA finds round structures called **ribosomes**. These organelles "read" the mRNA copy of the DNA blueprint and copy it again. This copy of a copy is the protein product. Depending on the cell type, the final product could be anything from a digestive enzyme to insulin.

The finished protein made in the endoplasmic reticulum is bundled up in a membrane sac called a **vesicle** and carried to its next stop, the **Golgi apparatus**. This is a sorting and packaging center that resembles a series of flat, stacked sacks. The Golgi apparatus manufactures large carbohydrate molecules which it then attaches to the protein products, forming **glycoproteins**. As more proteins enter, the flat sacs fill up and become more globular. The result is a ball of neatly packaged glycoproteins. They are sent to the cell membrane where they pass to the outside (are excreted). Then the sacs break open and their contents are released.

The energy for these activities and others is manufactured in the **mitochondria**, sausage-shaped organelles composed of two membranes. The outer membrane gives each mitochondrion a smooth appearance. The inner membrane contains many folds, and it is here that the enzymes used to produce energy are located. Mitochondria have their own DNA (genetic material) and their own protein-producing ribosomes. This has led many researchers to speculate that they are the descendants of bacteria that were swallowed but never digested by larger cells billions of years ago. Because mitochondrial DNA is passed from mother to daughter unchanged, it can be used to trace ancestry.

The digestive system of the cell is a collection of **lysosomes**. These are sacs that contain enzymes for digesting all of the major components of a cell. When an object—for example, a bacteria—gets inside of a cell, it is surrounded by a lysosome, which digests the intruder. Worn-out organelles also end up here so their parts can be recycled. Lysosomes can also burst and digest the cell they live in.

How Cells Divide

Different types of cells have different life spans, depending on their location and function. Some cells, such as neurons (nerve cells), are made to last a human lifetime. Others, like white blood cells, live for only two days. The cells that line the gastrointestinal tract live only for thirty-six hours before they are sloughed off. And just like people, cells can get sick and injured, causing death. For a tissue to function properly, damaged or dead cells must be replaced.

New cells are produced by the process of cell division, or **mitosis**, during which one parent cell divides into two identical daughter cells. A cell knows when to grow or divide by talking to its neighbors. A cell in a new neighborhood of rapidly growing tissue will get the go-ahead to propagate, while a cell in a crowded healthy tissue will be told more citizens are not welcome. Since a good cell citizen is a team player, it divides or travels only when the community deems it proper and necessary. When it reproduces independently or when it detaches from its neighbors, the cell is given a signal to self-destruct.

Cell division starts inside the nucleus, the cell's "brain." Inside the nucleus lie all of the coded instructions needed for the day-to-day life of the cell. These instructions are in the cell's genetic material, **deoxyribonucleic acid (DNA)**.

A DNA molecule (Figure 1.1) is elegantly simple. Often called the double helix, it resembles a long spiral ladder with one complete turn to every ten rungs. The backbones of the ladder are composed of deoxyriboses (a type of sugar) that alternate with phosphate groups. The rungs of the ladder are composed of molecules called **bases**. Each rung is composed of base pairs—two bases connected weakly in the center. The base pairs fit together like pieces of a jigsaw puzzle.

In humans, there are two types of bases. The purine bases, adenine and guanine, are made from the amino acid purine, and the pyrimidine bases, cytosine and thymine, are made from the amino acid pyrimidine. The purine base adenine always pairs with the pyrimidine base thymine, and the purine base guanine always pairs with the pyrimidine base cytosine. This means that if you were to look at the rungs in one DNA ladder, they might read adenine-thymine, guanine-cytosine, thymine-adenine;

Figure 1.1 DNA molecule

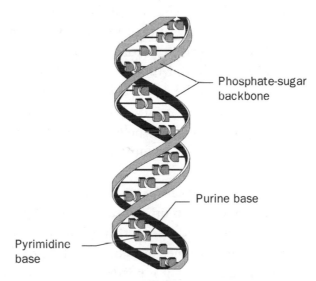

Phosphate-sugar backbone

Purine base

Pyrimidine base

and in another DNA molecule, they might read cytosine-guanine, adenine-thymine, cytosine-guanine. The sequence of the three base pairs forms a code word, or **codon**. In this way base pairs are letters, and codons are words. These letters and words form the language of life.

When a cell begins to divide, the DNA molecules coil into rod-shaped bodies called **chromosomes**. Each chromosome makes a duplicate of itself. On a molecular level this is accomplished by pulling the DNA ladder apart by the legs. The rungs separate at the weakest point, between the base pairs. Each half rebuilds into a whole molecule, using free bases floating in the nucleus. The result is two identical DNA molecules. During the last phase of cell duplication, the cell cytoplasm and cell membrane pinch inward between the two sets of chromosomes, forming two cells.

But not all duplications result in exact duplicates. Base pairs can be lost or placed in a different order. This is called a **mutation**. It results in lost words or sentences, misspelled codon words, or words being out of order in the cellular instructions. Mutations are not at all rare but are often minor, and the cell is able to get the gist of the instructions despite the errors. But occasionally a whole section of words is lost or misspelled into gibberish. When this happens to vital cell documents, the mutation causes death.

To prevent this, our cells have developed a backup system. Special enzymes zip up and down the DNA ladders, fixing misspelled words, something like a DNA spell-checker. But the spell-checker works well only when it is supplied with the enzymes it needs.

How Cells Die

Where there is birth, there must be death. A cell comes to the end of its life in one of two ways: necrosis or apoptosis. When bad things happen to good cells, the result is **necrosis**. This is a traumatic death from injury. It can be caused by accidents, lack of oxygen, cold temperature, or injury by bacterial or viral infections. Cancer can cause necrosis too. The cell that is injured swells and then bursts, spewing its organelles all over the tissue landscape. Cells killed in this way do not go out quietly. They make all the noise they can by sending message molecules to the cells nearby. When these messages are received, blood flow to the site of injury increases, causing swelling and redness. White blood cells pour into the area and devour the organelles and cellular debris until nothing of the injury is left. This process is called **inflammation**. It ensures that the damaged area is isolated from healthy tissue along with all the resources the body needs to return the area to health.

The other way a cell can die is called **apoptosis**. This is the quiet suicide that happens when a cell becomes worn out because it has reached the end of its life span, is damaged in the normal course of its life, or has just become superfluous. Apoptosis is sometimes called programmed cell death. A cell can decide to kill itself, internal reactive oxygen (a type of free radical damage) can trigger the process, or an outside agent (called a death activator) can cause the suicide. During apoptosis the cell shrinks and then breaks apart into small, neatly wrapped, membrane-covered pieces that are removed by white blood cells. No cellular contents leak into the tissues to cause inflammation, so the cell just silently disappears. Apoptotic death is a fact of life. It happens a hundred million times each day in your body. In less than two years a cell mass equal to your body weight is replaced through apoptosis. When normal apoptosis is prevented, the result can be cancer. Cells that should die because their DNA is damaged continue to grow. Some chemotherapy drugs work by triggering apoptosis in cancer cells.

Tissues

So far we have talked about the individual cell, but your cells do not live separate lives. Each of your cell citizens belongs to a tissue, a community of physically similar cells. Cell citizens of the same tissue type belong to a sort of family or union. They may not live in the same neighborhood or town, but they look alike and perform the same job. There are four main types of tissue: epithelial tissue, connective tissue, muscle tissue, and nervous tissue. Cancers are named after the type of tissue from which they develop, as well as the location of the tumor.

Cancer cells and tumors share many of the characteristics of the tissues from which they originate. The type of cell the cancer originated from and the type of cells it is growing with determine the type and length of treatment.

Epithelial Tissue

Most of the cells you can see on your body are **epithelial cells**. Cells in this clan earn their living by covering, lining, secreting, and absorbing. Wherever your body comes into contact with the outside environment, epithelial tissue can be found. It covers all of the external parts of your body from hair to toenails, lines the cavities of body organs, and forms the inner lining of the body cavities. The gastrointestinal tract from mouth to anus is lined with epithelial tissue. So is the respiratory system. The insides of the uterus, bladder, and all blood vessels are lined with epithelial tissue.

There are two kinds of epithelial tissue: glandular and membranous. **Glandular epithelial tissue** contains small **exocrine glands** (glands that release their products through ducts). These glands secrete various substances into the environment, organ cavity, or body cavity. In the gastrointestinal tract, for instance, glandular epithelial cells make the passage of food and waste products easier by secreting a lubricating mucus. In the stomach they secrete hydrochloric acid and the intrinsic factor necessary for vitamin B_{12} absorption.

Membranous epithelial tissues serve as coverings or linings. These cells are classified according to their shape and type of cell layer.

- Membranous cells come in three shapes. Squamous cells are flat and scalelike. Cuboidal cells are cube shaped and have more cytoplasm. Columnar cells are taller than they are wide and look like standing columns.

- Membranous cells come in four types of cell layers. Simple epithelium is only one layer deep. Stratified epithelium is layered one cell on top of another. Pseudostratified columnar epithelium gives the appearance of having more than one cell layer but is actually only one layer deep. Transitional epithelium is composed of differing cell shapes which are layered.

Put these two classifications together for the various types of membranous epithelial cells. For example, simple squamous epithelium is composed of flat cells one layer deep. Substances easily cross this kind of tissue. Stratified transitional epithelium has the ability to stretch and so lines the bladder.

Epithelial cells are **avascular**, meaning they do not have a blood supply. When they die, they slough off. A good example of this is the gradual shedding of skin cells or the not-so-gradual shedding of dandruff. Cancer cells in epithelial tissue also can shed, making them easy to collect and examine. This is useful for diagnosis, because cancer cells have a very distinctive appearance under the microscope. The familiar Pap smear is a good example of how shed cells can be useful in cancer diagnosis. It is performed by taking a smear of shed uterine cells from the cervix.

Epithelial cells must divide very quickly to replace cells lost to wear and tear. Therefore, cancer treatments (such as chemotherapy and radiation), which target rapidly dividing cancer cells, will also affect epithelial tissue. At least 85 percent of all cancers originate in the epithelial tissue. Cancerous tumors of the surface epithelium are called **carcinomas**. Those of the glandular epithelium are called **adenocarcinomas**.

Examples of Malignant Tumors

Carcinomas
(Cancers Originating in the Epithelial Tissue)

Type	Location
Adenocarcinoma	Gland
Adenocarcinoma of the lung	Lung glandular tissue
Gastric adenocarcinoma	Stomach glandular epithelium
Pancreatic carcinoma	Pancreas
Papillocarcinoma	Epithelial tissue
Melanoma	Skin

Sarcomas
(Cancers Originating in the Bone and Soft Tissues)

Type	Location
Fibrosarcoma	Fibrous tissue
Hemangiosarcoma	Blood vessels
Chondrosarcoma	Cartilage
Synovial sarcoma	Synovial tissue (lining of the joints)
Osteosarcoma	Bone
Liposarcoma	Fat
Leiomyosarcoma	Smooth muscle
Rhabdomyosarcoma	Striated muscle

Leukemias
(Malignancies of the Leukocytes, or White Blood Cells)

Type	Cell Affected/Origin
Acute lymphocytic leukemia (all)	Lymphocytes
Chronic lymphocytic leukemia (cll)	Lymphocytes
Acute myelogenous leukemia (aml)	Bone marrow
Chronic myelogenous leukemia (cml)	Bone marrow
Chronic lymphoid leukemia (cll)	Lymphoid cells
Erythroleukemia	Erythrocytic tissue
Myelocytic leukemia	Granulocytic tissue
Reticuloendotheliosis (hairy cell leukemia)	Lymphoid cells

Lymphomas
(Connective Tissue Cancers of the Lymph System)

Type	Tissue Affected
Hodgkin's disease	Lymph nodes
Malignant granuloma	Lymph nodes
Lymphogranuloma	Lymph nodes

Cancers of the Nervous Tissue
(Named After the Type of Cell in Which They Occur)

Type	Location
Glioma	Glial tissue
Neurilemmic sarcoma	Nerve sheaths
Astrocytomas	Astrocytes (a type of neuroglial cell)
Retinoblastoma	Retina
Meningeal sarcoma	Meninges (the membranes that cover the brain and spinal cord)

Other Malignancies

Type	Tissue Affected/ Tissue of Origin
Multiple myeloma	Plasma cells and bone marrow
Choriocarcinoma	Placenta (germ cell tumor)
Dysgerminoma	Ovary (germ cell tumor)
Seminoma	Testis (germ cell tumor)
Thyoma	Thymus

Endothelial Tissue

Blood and lymph vessels are lined with a very special type of simple squamous epithelium called the endothelium. Cells in this tissue serve as the leaders and the gatekeepers. Most of us have never heard of the endothelium, yet in our bodies it is this tissue layer that makes important decisions, gives orders, and coordinates actions. It does this by releasing countless types of chemical messengers that tell nearby and faraway cells what to do. Physically it serves as the blood-brain barrier that decides what does and does not get into that important organ. Despite their importance, however, endothelial cells are so fragile they are often called the Achilles' heel of the cardiovascular system. They can be easily damaged by chemotherapy and radiation.

Endothelial cells can live from months to years, a very long lifespan when compared with other epithelial cells. This means they are not affected by chemotherapy in the same way as the other fast-growing types of epithelial cells. Instead, chemotherapy can cause endothelial cells to become reactive—a term which means that the cells overreact to situations. For example, chemotherapy can change how the endothelium reacts with platelets, the blood elements involved in blood-clot formation. This happens in breast cancer patients and can result in blood clots. The tendency to overreact can last long after the cancer treatment is finished.

Since the endothelium is part of the cardiovascular system we will go into more detail when we discuss this system in the next chapter.

Connective Tissue

Connective tissue forms the delicate webs, fluid blood, and hard bones used to connect, support, transport, and defend the body. It is a complex of live cells separated by various types of fibers embedded in a nonliving material called the **matrix**, or ground substance. The type of matrix material and fiber determines what kind of characteristic the connective tissue exhibits. For example, cartilage tissue has a gellike matrix, bone tissue has a hard mineral matrix, and blood tissue has a liquid matrix.

Connective tissue can be divided into a variety of types, some of which overlap. They include the following:

- Loose ordinary connective or **areolar tissue** connects tissues and organs by acting as a flexible glue. Its matrix is a soft, viscous gel.

- **Adipose connective tissue** resembles areolar tissue with the addition of adipose (fat storage) cells. It forms protective pads around the kidneys and other organs and serves as body insulation.

- **Dense fibrous connective tissue** is made up of a mix of collagen and elastic fibers in a liquid matrix. It forms tendons and ligaments and is also found in the dermal layer of the skin. Scars are made of this type of tissue. It offers a flexible but strong connection between bone and muscle tissues.

- **Reticular tissue** is composed of reticular cells that coat slender, branching reticular fibers, forming a three-dimensional network. Reticular tissue forms the scaffold of the spleen, lymph nodes, and thymus and so is an important part of the immune system. The meshlike qualities of this tissue allow the organs to filter harmful substances and cells from the blood and lymph.

- **Bone (osseous) tissue** is made up of osteocytes embedded in a matrix of collagen fibers and mineral salts. The mineral salts give bones their hardness.

- **Cartilage** consists of chondrocytes embedded in a flexible gristlike matrix. Your earlobes contain elastic cartilage, your knee contains fibrocartilage, and your respiratory tubes are held open by rings of hyaline cartilage. Cartilage tissue has no blood supply, so nutrients must diffuse in. For this reason, tears in cartilage do not heal quickly or well.

- **Myeloid tissue** forms the bone marrow and cells derived from it, including the red blood cells and platelets, as well as the granulocytes and monocytes needed for the immune system.

- **Blood tissue** is the most unusual connective tissue. It is in a liquid form and so does not contain any fibers or a ground substance. Blood tissue has two components: the liquid part, called **plasma**, and the solid cellular part, which contains the red blood cells (**erythrocytes**), the platelets, and the white blood cells (**leukocytes**) of the immune system.

Cancers that occur in the bone and the soft tissues (connective and muscle) are called **sarcomas**. Sarcomas are most common in children. Cancers of the lymphatic system are called **lymphomas**. Lymphomas can arise anywhere in the lymph system, but most commonly occur in the lymph nodes. **Multiple myeloma** is a cancer of the plasma cells. **Leukemias** are cancers of the blood-forming tissues. They affect both the ability of the cell to mature and the ability of the cell to perform its function.

Muscle Tissue

Muscle cells are the expert movers of the body. They can be divided into three types:

- Skeletal muscle tissue attaches to bones and moves the skeleton. It is sometimes referred to as "striated muscle" because under a microscope the cell fibers have cross stripes or as "voluntary muscle" because you can move it at will.

- Visceral muscle tissue is found in the soft internal organs of the body (the viscera). It is sometimes referred to as "smooth muscle" because of its lack of cross stripes or as "involuntary muscle" because it is not ordinarily controlled by will.

- Cardiac muscle tissue forms the walls of the heart. It is an involuntary muscle with many of the attributes of striated muscle.

Sarcomas of the muscle tissue usually occur in children. Cancer of the striated muscle is the fifth most common cancer in children after leukemia and lymphoma, central nervous system tumors, neuroblastoma, and Wilms' tumor.

Nervous Tissue

Nervous tissue forms the organs of the brain, spinal cord, and nerves. Nerve cells are the telephone and data communication workers of the body. They make electronic communications possible. There are two types of nervous tissue:

- Nerve cells, or **neurons**, are the cells that actually perform the transmissions. Neurons have a cell body, called the soma; one axon, which can be as long as one meter; and one or more dendrites (nerve fibers).

- **Neuroglia cells** support and connect the neurons. For example, Schwann cells make up the neurilemma and myelin coats of neurons. Astrocytes form tight webs around the capillaries in the brain. Together with the capillary walls, they form the **blood-brain barrier**, the structure responsible for keeping most larger molecules out of the brain.

Tumors occurring inside the skull (intracranial) are named after the type of cell from which they developed. Examples are astrocytomas (from astrocytes), glioblastomas (from neuroglia cells), and melanomas (from melanocytes).

Tumors of the central nervous system are the most common type of solid tumor in children. In adults many intracranial malignacies are cancers that have spread from a distant site (secondary tumors from metastasis).

Cells, like people, contain a number of specialized structures. Each structure, or organelle, performs a specific job.

The cell's activities are directed by the nucleus, which contains the genetic material. When a cell divides, the genetic material divides. When errors occur in this process, the result is a mutation.

Like a union, each tissue is composed of one type of cell that has its own size and character. And like a union, each tissue has a specific area of expertise. Epithelial tissue covers, lines, secretes, and absorbs. Connective tissue supports, connects, and protects from foreign invaders. Muscle tissue specializes in producing movement. Nervous tissue specializes in communication. In the next chapter, you'll find out about organs and organ systems.

2

Organs and Organ Systems

As cancer progresses from one cell into a tumor, it changes the organ's ability to function and disrupts the entire system to which the organ belongs. This chapter will help you understand the basic anatomy of the body and the organization of your organs.

Each of your cell citizens lives in a town. Some of the towns, such as the brain, heart, liver, and skin, are very large and perform an indispensable service. The great city of your heart, for example, is where large numbers of the muscle family live and work. These cells enjoy the harried existence of life in an essential organ. Other cells fancy the simple life of the heart suburbs, in the arteries and veins of the limbs. They prefer the reduced-stress lifestyle of nonessential organs. Each organ-town is a composite of several different types of tissues. And even though the cells look different and come from different tissues, they all work together toward a common goal.

Each town and city also belongs to a larger organization with the same mission. Organ systems are composed of varying numbers and types of organs. They act together to perform a necessary job for the body. Each organ in the organ system depends upon the others, and each organ system is closely related to the other organ systems. For example, in the musculoskeletal system the skeleton is responsible for allowing the body to move. But it cannot provide the movement itself; for that function it must rely on the muscles. Working together, they get the body from here to there. The musculoskeletal system also works with other organ systems. Within the long bones and pelvis lie the yellow bone marrow of the immune system and the red bone marrow of the blood system.

There are ten major organ systems: the cardiovascular (or circulatory) system, integumentary system, skeletal system, muscular system, respiratory system, digestive system, nervous system, endocrine system, reproductive system, and urinary system. The immune system is different from the organ systems because it is made up of individual cells rather than organs. We will examine it separately.

Cardiovascular or Circulatory System

Each cell and organ is connected to its fellow cells and organs through the cardiovascular system. This is the transportation network, a living river that circulates through a complex series of interconnected canals. These canals pulse to the rhythm of the heart—contracting and dilating to direct blood flow and regulate blood pressure. The circulatory system is why no organ is independent of another. We are literally stitched together with thousands and thousands of miles of blood vessels. It is the circulatory system that binds our separate parts into one organism. The cardiovascular system has four main components: blood (a liquid tissue), the heart that pumps the blood, the vessels through which the blood flows, and the endothelium that controls it all.

Blood is the familiar salty red liquid that serves as the carrier in the cardiovascular system. The liquid part of blood, plasma, contains a vast and varied number of dissolved substances, including vitamins, minerals, and other nutrients; blood sugar (glucose); insulin and other hormones used for communication; salts; enzymes; waste products from cells; and gases. Suspended in the plasma is the solid portion of blood. It consists of the hemoglobin-containing red blood cells responsible for oxygen transport, the white blood cells of the immune system, and the platelets involved in blood-clot formation.

The heart is at once the beginning and the end of the cardiovascular system. Made almost entirely of muscle, it functions as a four-chambered pump propelling oxygen-depleted blood from the tissues into the lungs. There the carbon dioxide from the tissues is exchanged for oxygen and the blood returns to the heart, which then pumps it out through the arteries. Your heart will beat approximately three billion times in your lifetime. Blood travels through a series of tunnels called the blood vessels. The arteries carry oxygen-rich blood away from the heart to the tissues. The veins carry oxygen-depleted blood away from the tissues back to the heart. It is in the capillaries, the smallest blood vessels, where hungry tissues exchange carbon dioxide waste for oxygen. The oxygen-poor blood then drains into the veins.

The brain of the cardiovascular system is the **endothelium**. This is the single layer of cells that lines the arteries. The smallest arteries are the arterioles, which are little more than the endothelium surrounded by muscle fibers and a membrane. As the arterioles become the capillaries, they shed the muscles, leaving only the endothelium and the membrane. It is in the capillary bed that messages carried in the blood are delivered. Oxygen and other nutrients are exchanged for carbon dioxide and other waste products. Almost every cell in your body is next to a capillary. For years the endothelium was thought to be little more than a passive barrier between blood and blood vessel. Today medical researchers know that it is the brain of the cardiovascular system, capable of secreting a wide range of hormones and other messenger molecules. Inside the blood vessel, the endothelium uses these messenger molecules to direct blood flow, blood pressure, and viscosity and to regulate blood vessel growth. Outside the vessel, it controls and regulates each organ's environment, the disposal of its toxins and waste, and its exposure to drugs and access to oxygen and other nutrients.

No cell in the human body escapes the endothelium's control. Ever vigilant, it is a hidden surveillance system that penetrates every nook and cranny of our bodies. This single layer of cells might sound small, but when taken together, the endothelial organ has a mass equal to that of five hearts, an area large enough to cover six tennis courts, and a weight greater than that of the liver. It is the endo-thelium that is intimately involved with tumor growth and spread. Tumors cannot grow beyond 2 millimeters (less than one-tenth of an inch) without growing more blood vessels. This process of sprouting new blood vessels from established ones is called **angiogenesis**.

The Integumentary System

The "integument" is another name for the skin, and the integumentary system includes the skin and its various attachments, including hair, finger- and toenails, lips, and skin glands. It is made up of a surface epithelial tissue lying atop a base of connective tissue. In a general way, the skin's job is to keep the inside in and the outside out. Skin cells keep you watertight. Your skin prevents your bathwater from swelling you up like a sponge and your sunlamp from shriveling you into a raisin. Your skin protects your insides from the environment. Your skin cell citizens prevent the illegal immigration of the vast majority of bacteria and viruses and block the entry of toxic chemicals.

The skin has other functions as well. It regulates body temperature through perspiration; manufactures important chemicals such as vitamin D; and acts as a sensory organ for heat, cold, touch, pressure, and pain. The skin also excretes substances through your glands and pores; these substances include salts of various types and water.

Because the skin is exposed to many environmental factors, it is the most common site on the human body to form cancer. The types of skin cancer that occur most frequently are basal and squamous cell cancers caused by exposure to ultraviolet light. Melanoma, the more serious form of skin cancer, develops from melanocytes, the pigment–producing cells.

The Skeletal System

The skull, spine, rib cage, arm and leg bones, ligaments, tendons, and joints are included in the skeletal system (Figure 2.1). It is almost entirely composed of two types of connective tissue: bone and cartilage. This system performs three major jobs:

- The joints, or articulations, in the skeleton give the body the ability to move.
- The bone tissue serves as a bank. Minerals such as calcium, magnesium, and phosphate can be deposited in the matrix and withdrawn when needed.
- Hidden away in the safe-deposit box inside the bone is the red bone marrow. This tissue, a part of the blood system, is where red blood cells are made in the vital process called **hemopoiesis**.

Sarcomas of the bone tissue are rare and usually affect young persons. Most other cancers do not begin in the bone but have traveled (metastasized) there from other organs.

Figure 2.1 Skeletal and muscular systems

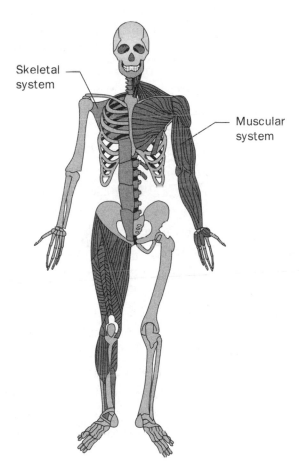

Skeletal
system

Muscular
system

Muscular System

Muscle tissue can be organized into separate muscles that
are considered individual organs. Together, they form the
muscular system (see Figure 2.1). The cells in a muscle
have two major duties: movement and heat production.

Although the joints of the skeletal system allow movement, they cannot make the movement themselves. For this they require the contraction of striated muscle. Movement inside the body cavity is provided by muscles made up of smooth muscle cells. For example, the movement of food through the digestive tract is provided by the smooth muscles in the esophagus, stomach, and intestines. Urine is moved through the urinary system by smooth muscles in the ureters, bladder, and urethra. Air is moved in and out of the lungs by smooth muscle in the diaphragm. The muscular system also serves as the major heat generator for the body, keeping tissues warm.

Muscle is made almost entirely of protein. When protein intake through food is low or when food protein is not digested or absorbed properly, it must come from some other source. That source is the muscle tissue. Even when enough protein is provided by the diet, cancer cells will raid the muscles for protein to change into glucose. When muscle tissue decreases, the individual muscle is less able to perform its job, causing weakness in movement and the sensation of coldness due to loss of heat production. Although cancer of the muscular system is very rare, cancer in general can cause a serious loss of muscle tissue.

Nervous System

The brain, spinal cord, and nerves are the organs of the nervous system (Figure 2.2). This system consists primarily of nervous tissue supported and protected by connective tissue.

Figure 2.2 The brain

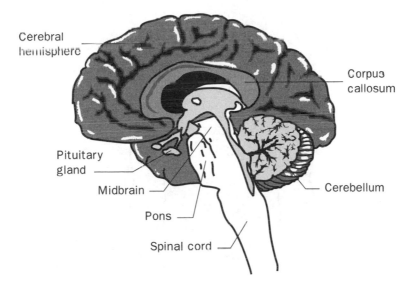

The cell citizens of your nervous system work in several critical jobs. They are responsible for rapid cell-to-cell and organ-to-organ communication. Cells in these organs produce **neurotransmitters**, which initiate and sustain electrical impulses. This allows your brain to talk to organs far and near, controlling, coordinating, and integrating their work. These messages travel very fast and provide only brief control. Nervous system cells also function as sensors. They are able to recognize heat, light, pressure, and temperature.

Cancers of the nervous system can be found in the gray matter of the brain, on the membrane covering the brain, and in the spinal cord. Endocrine glands located in the brain may also be a source of tumors. The skull is a common site for secondary tumors that have migrated from their place of origin.

Figure 2.3 Endocrine system

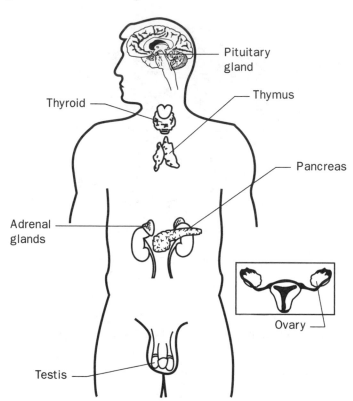

Endocrine System

The endocrine system (Figure 2.3) includes the pituitary and pineal glands; the hypothalamus, thyroid, and adrenal glands; the pancreas; and the testes or ovaries and placenta. These glands release their hormones into the bloodstream directly, as opposed to the exocrine glands, which release their products into ducts.

The cell citizens of an endocrine gland are writers. They compose messages called **hormones**, which are distributed primarily through the bloodstream. Glands perform the same job as the nervous system: communication, integration, and control of bodily functions. The signals travel slower but are much longer lasting. Hormones are the main regulators of metabolism, growth and development, and reproduction.

Endocrine cell tumors are called **carcinoids**. Cancers of the endocrine system include the following:

- Germ cell cancers—these include testicular cancer (male), gestational trophoblastic neoplasms (placental), and ovarian cancer (female).
- Pancreatic cancer—more than 90 percent of the carcinomas of the pancreas are mucinous adenocarcinomas that originate in the pancreatic duct.
- Thyroid cancer

Because they stimulate abnormal hormone production, cancers of the endocrine system are often able to produce symptoms in distant sites.

Lymphatic System

The lymphatic system (Figure 2.4) is made up of the lymphatic vessels, lymph nodes, lymph, thymus, and spleen. It transports fluids, large molecules, fat, and fat-related nutrients; it is also involved in the workings of the immune system. Patches of lymphatic tissue are also found in isolated areas in the gastrointestinal tract, lungs, and bone marrow. The system provides a means of returning liquid that escapes from the blood into the body tissues.

Figure 2.4 Lymphatic system

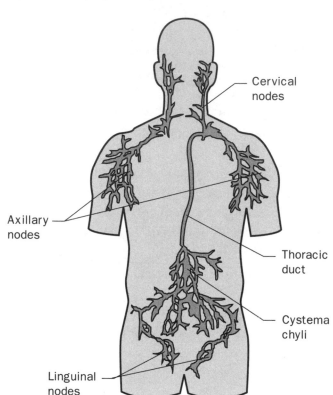

The lymph nodes (Figure 2.5) are a combination police station and barracks. Round or kidney-shaped, these structures are usually found in groups around the body. You have between five hundred and fifteen hundred lymph nodes that range in size from very tiny to about one inch in diameter. When nodes in the neck, armpits, or groin are enlarged, they can be felt. This is why your doctor pokes around your neck and abdomen.

The lymph system is used by the cells of the immune system. When an attacker such as a bacterium, virus, or

Figure 2.5 Location of lymph nodes in the head and neck

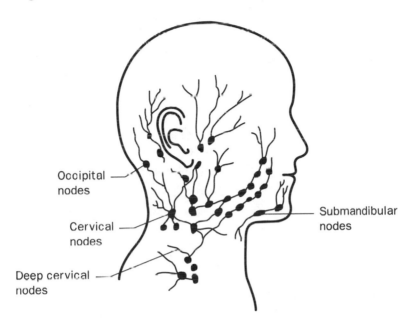

cancer cell is picked up by one of the white blood cells, it is brought to the lymph node to be imprisoned and studied. When large numbers of these troublemakers are incarcerated, or when the immune army beefs up its security due to a threat, the bulging barracks can be felt by the doctor. Sometimes these nodes are removed via surgery. They are examined under a microscope to see if any cancer cells are present in the "jail." If the node has no cancer cells inside, your doctor knows that the cancer has not reached as far as the area drained by those nodes.

The organs involved in blood cell formation are a common site for cancer development. These types of cancer are called leukemias. Cancers of the lymph system are called lymphomas. (The sidebar in the preceding chapter listed common lymphatic cancers.)

Respiratory System

The cells in your respiratory system (Figure 2.6) are responsible for the exchange of carbon dioxide and oxygen between the air and the blood. Its organs include the nose, pharynx (throat), larynx, trachea, bronchi, and lungs.

Respiration involves two parallel processes. During external respiration (lung breathing), oxygen-rich air is brought into the lungs when you inhale, and carbon dioxide is removed from the body when you exhale. Through internal respiration (tissue breathing), oxygen in the red blood cells is exchanged for the waste carbon dioxide in the tissues.

When you inhale, the air is filtered and warmed by the nasal cavity and pharynx, then passes over the larynx on its way to the trachea. The trachea is composed of smooth muscle embedded with C-shaped cartilage rings, which function to keep the airway open at all times. As the trachea enters the chest, it divides into two branches called the **bronchi**, one of which leads to the right lung and the other to the left lung. Each of the bronchi divides into **bronchioles**, which end in the **alveoli** (air sacs). Each alveolus resembles a small balloon that expands and contracts with the inhalation and exhalation of air. Beneath the thin membranes of the alveoli lie the capillary beds where the oxygen is collected by the red blood cells. Blood leaving the lungs is pulled into the heart and then pumped out through the arteries to oxygen-needy tissues.

Your two lungs are divided into lobes. The right lung has three lobes: upper, middle, and lower. The left lung has only two lobes: upper and lower. Between the lungs is the **mediastinum**, a cavity that contains the heart, aorta, esophagus, trachea, and bronchi. Each lung is covered by

Figure 2.6 Respiratory system

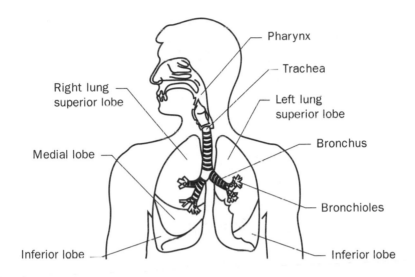

two membranes: the outer layer (called the parietal pleura) and the inner layer that lies on top of the lung (called the visceral pleura). The chest cavity is divided from the abdominal cavity by a muscular partition called the **diaphragm**. By contracting and relaxing, the diaphragm provides the pressure needed for respiration.

Each day your respiratory organs are exposed to more than 10,000 liters of air containing toxins, dust, microorganisms, and other hazardous airborne particles. This makes those organs common sites for cancer. Carcinomas of the lung can be divided into four types:

- Squamous cell carcinoma (30 to 35 percent of cases)
- Adenocarcinoma (35 to 40 percent of cases)
- Large-cell carcinoma (about 10 percent of cases)
- Small-cell carcinoma (about 20 to 25 percent of cases)

These types are commonly grouped as small-cell carcinomas and non–small-cell carcinomas.

Lung cancer is the leading cause of cancer deaths in the United States. A joint report from the American Cancer Society, the Centers for Disease Control and Prevention, the National Cancer Institute, and the North American Association of Central Cancer Registries estimates that about 174,000 Americans will be diagnosed with lung cancer in 2006.

The Digestive System

The digestive system (Figure 2.7) consists of the mouth, pharynx (throat), esophagus, stomach, intestines, rectum, and anus. These organs form a long, open-ended tube called the **alimentary canal**, or the **gastrointestinal (GI) tract**. Accessory organs include the teeth, tongue, salivary glands, liver, gallbladder, and pancreas. The digestive tract breaks down food, absorbs nutrients, and eliminates feces (bodily waste). The entire alimentary canal is lined with epithelial cells. When the replacement of these fast-growing cells is halted as a result of chemotherapy or radiation, painful side effects such as mouth sores, sore throat, and stomach upset can result. Damage to the epithelium of the small intestine, however, causes more than just discomfort. It can result in electrolyte loss through diarrhea or malnutrition from malabsorption.

The main function of the epithelium of the small intestine is to absorb nutrients. This is reflected in its unusual structure. The lining of the small intestine looks like the

Figure 2.7 Digestive system

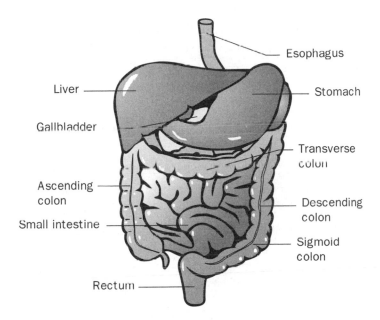

scrunched-up sleeve of a velvet shirt; its velvety, circular folds are covered with millions of small fingerlike projections called **villi**. Each villus is 1 millimeter in height and has a small artery, a vein, and a lymph vessel running through its center. It is covered with a single layer of cells that have even finer projections on their top exposed surfaces called **microvilli**. It's hard to imagine something so thin, but each cell on the villus has about seventeen hundred of these tiny hairs sprouting from its "head." Under the microscope, the microvilli projecting out from the end of each villus give the appearance of a paintbrush and are referred to as the "brush border." Enzymes necessary to digest foods are produced in the brush border near the top of each villi. The digested nutrients then pass through the villi walls into the blood or lymph vessels. This arrangement of villi and microvilli increases the absorptive area of the small intestine to about 250 square meters, the size of a small tennis court.

When cancer treatments such as radiation or chemotherapy injure the cells of the villi, some nutrients can no longer be digested (due to the loss of the enzymes) or absorbed (due to the loss of the microvilli and villi). This can result in malnutrition.

Since the digestive system is open to the environment and its toxins, it is a common site for cancer development. We will divide it into four parts: the mouth and related structures; the esophagus, stomach, and small intestine; the colon; and the liver and related structures.

Cancers of the Upper Aerodigestive Tract

The upper aerodigestive tract includes the structures you use to eat and breathe, including the lips, mouth, tongue, nose, nasal sinuses, throat, salivary glands, and neck. Squamous cell carcinoma is by far the most common type of cancer to occur in this area. This type of cancer is strongly related to exposure to environmental toxins such as alcohol, tobacco leaves or smoke, and industrial chemicals. Since all of the surfaces in touch with the toxins are at risk, once a cancer develops on one structure, it is not uncommon to find independent lesions on other nearby surfaces. To prevent the disease from recurring and to allow the epithelial tissues to become healthy again, you must stop the exposure to the toxins.

Sometimes surgery to remove cancerous lesions can result in eating difficulties. When this occurs, it is important that you see a certified nutritionist or dietitian to help you get the nourishment your body needs to heal itself.

Cancers of the Esophagus, Stomach, and Small Intestine

Half of esophageal cancers occur in the middle third of the organ, with the remainder evenly divided between the upper and lower thirds. Most cancers of the first two segments are squamous cell carcinomas. Those in the lower third are usually adenocarcinomas. Gastric cancers (*gastric* means "of the stomach") are usually adenocarcinomas. Cancers of the small intestine are very rare. They are usually carcinoids, developed from the endocrine cells scattered throughout the small intestine, or lymphomas, developed from the lymphoid cells in the intestine.

Colorectal Cancers

Malignancies of the colon, rectum, and anus are classified as colorectal cancers. The colon is the most common site for tumors in the gastrointestinal tract. The American Cancer Society estimates that there are approximately 151,000 new cases of colorectal cancer each year in the United States. Ninety-eight percent of colorectal cancers are carcinomas, with 60 to 70 percent occurring in the lower third of the colon and rectum.

Liver and Biliary Tract Cancers

The liver is the largest glandular organ of your body, over-seeing and managing the internal environment. It has a wide variety of jobs:

- It receives, via the portal vein, all of the nutrient-rich blood from the intestines and is involved in fat, protein, and carbohydrate metabolism.
- It is responsible for detoxifying (making harmless) a wide variety of substances.
- It serves as a storehouse for excess vitamins B_{12}, A, and D and the mineral iron.
- It is an exocrine gland, producing about a pint of bile each day. Bile works as an emulsifier, allowing fats and fat-soluble nutrients to dissolve in the watery lymph.

Without an adequate supply of bile, fat is not absorbed properly (a condition called steatorrhea).

Because its job is so important, the liver has a tremendous ability to regenerate. If large areas of cells are killed or removed but the remaining section is healthy, the liver will regrow and resume most of its functions.

The biliary system includes the **gallbladder**, which stores the bile made in the liver, and the ducts of the liver, gallbladder, and pancreas. The right and left extrahepatic ducts exit the liver and then join to form the common hepatic duct. These ducts carry bile. The cystic duct from the gallbladder joins the common hepatic duct to form the common bile duct. Bile can either leave the gallbladder through the cystic duct on its way to the duodenum or enter the gallbladder, where it is stored until needed. The common bile duct is joined by the pancreatic duct carrying digestive enzymes just before entering the duodenum at a nipplelike structure called ampulla of Vater.

The most commonly occurring cancer of the liver is hepatocellular carcinoma. However, most hepatic (liver) cancers are metastases from primary tumors of the breast, lung, and gastrointestinal tract. Biliary tract cancers include periampullary cancer and carcinomas of the gallbladder and extrahepatic biliary ducts.

Urinary System

The job of cleaning up the bloodstream falls to the cells of the urinary system (Figure 2.8), which includes a pair of kidneys and ureters, the bladder, and the urethra. Together, the fist-sized kidneys filter more than 1,700 liters of blood each day to produce about 1 liter of highly concentrated urine. Urine can be compared to used bathwater. It contains the waste products that have been dumped into the bloodstream by other organs. Urine drips from the kidney down through a long tube called the ureter until it reaches the bladder. The bladder is a hollow muscular organ that expands as it fills with urine. Urine is temporarily stored here, exiting through the urethra during micturition (urination). The kidneys also aid in maintaining the balance of electrolytes, water, and acid.

The most common cancers of the kidneys are renal cell carcinoma (also called hypernephroma or adenocarcinoma of the kidney), which accounts for 85 to 90 percent of all

Figure 2.8 Urinary system

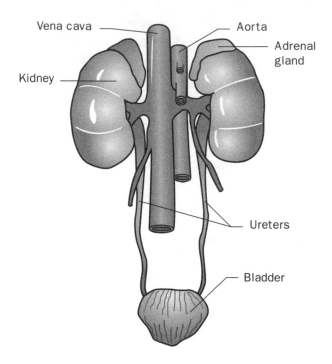

Vena cava — Aorta

Adrenal gland

Kidney

Ureters

Bladder

renal (kidney) cancers; Wilms' tumor (also called nephro-blastoma), which is a childhood tumor; and urothelial carcinomas of the renal pelvis. Cancers of the ureters are rare and are usually secondary tumors from metastasis. The most common forms of bladder cancer are transitional cell carcinoma, which accounts for 90 percent of bladder carcinomas; squamous cell carcinoma; and mixed transitional and squamous cell carcinoma. Adenomas of the bladder are rare and include signet cell carcinoma and mesonephric or nephrogenic adenoma. Secondary tumors can also occur from cancers in the cervix, uterus, prostate, and rectum. Most cancers of the urethra are squamous cell cancers.

Male Reproductive System

The male reproductive system (Figure 2.9) includes the male gonads or testes, where sperm is manufactured; genital ducts (epididymis, vas deferens, ejaculatory ducts, and urethra); and the supporting structures (scrotum, penis, and spermatic cords). The cells of the male reproductive system are dedicated to the manufacture, transport, and introduction of sperm into the female tract.

Testes and Epididymis

The **testes** are a pair of organs located in an external sac called the **scrotum**. They are both a production site for

Figure 2.9 Male reproductive system

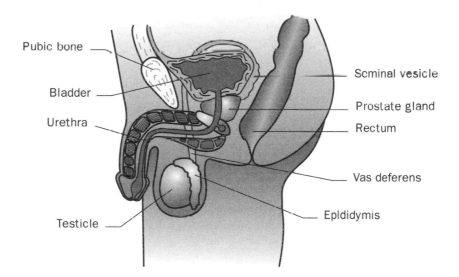

sperm and glands that secrete the male hormone, testosterone. Sperm created in the testes exit through the **epididymis**, a very long but thin, tightly coiled tube. Here the sperm are allowed to mature for one to three weeks before passing through the ejaculatory duct in the penis. The genital ducts are surrounded by a layer of tough connective tissue.

More than 95 percent of testicular malignancies are **germ** cell cancers. Germ cell cancer can be divided into two major types: seminomas and nonseminomatous germ cell tumors, including embryonal carcinomas, yolk sac tumors, choriocarcinomas, teratomas, and tumors that are a combination of these types.

Prostate

The prostate is a doughnut-shaped gland that surrounds the urethra. It produces a thin alkaline substance that forms the largest part of the seminal fluid. Carcinoma of the prostate is the most common form of cancer in men. More than 100,000 new cases are detected each year.

Penis

The two types of penile cancer are carcinoma of the penis and carcinoma in situ, a type of carcinoma in which the malignant cells have not penetrated into the adjacent tissues or metastasized to distant sites.

Female Reproductive System

The female reproductive system (Figure 2.10) includes the female gonads (ovaries), the genital ducts (uterus, fallopian tubes, and vagina), and the supporting structures (**mammary glands**, or breasts (Figure 2.11), and **vulva**, or genitalia). The female tract manufactures the ova (eggs); accepts sperm; fosters fertilization; and allows development, birth, and nourishment of the offspring.

Breast cancer is the most common malignancy in women of the Western world. According to the American Cancer Society, approximately 143,000 new cases are diagnosed each year. Cancers of the breast include infil-

Figure 2.10 Female reproductive system

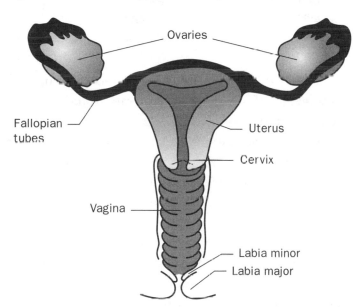

Figure 2.11 Side view of the breast

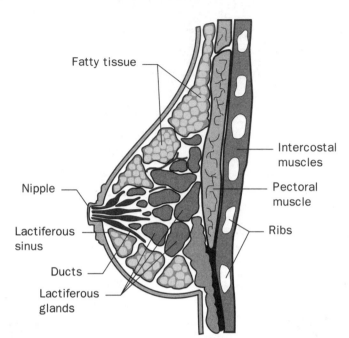

Fatty tissue

Intercostal muscles

Nipple

Pectoral muscle

Lactiferous sinus

Ribs

Ducts

Lactiferous glands

trating ductal carcinoma, infiltrating lobular carcinoma, cystosarcoma phylloides, and intraductal carcinoma (ductal carcinoma in situ, or DCIS).

Malignancies associated with the genital tract include invasive squamous cell carcinomas of the cervix, vulva, and vagina; clear cell adenocarcinomas of the vagina; endometrial carcinoma; and choriocarcinoma.

Cancers of the ovary include epithelial carcinomas (serous, endometroid, clear cell, and mucinous); malignant germ cell tumors (dysgerminoma, yolk sac tumor, and immature teratoma); and sex cord stromal (granulosa cell) tumors. The growth of healthy reproductive tissue is regulated by the sex hormones. Unfortunately, cancers arising from these tissues will also respond to hormones by increasing the rate at which they grow.

Tissues are organized into organs that perform a specific function. This is much like a city where several unions (tissues) supply workers dedicated to a common function. The organs of the body are further organized into organ systems or industries: groups of cities and towns that produce similar products or services. There are ten major organ systems in the human body. What affects one organ will affect the entire organ system and thus the ability of that system to do its part in tissue production and maintenance.

3

Cancer:
When Good Cells Go Bad

An understanding of cancer growth and tumors requires knowledge of how a normal cell is transformed into a malignant cell. This chapter will follow the life a single cancer cell from the beginning to its transformation to its spread to other organs. It is important to understand the stages of cancer development because they hold the key to treatment.

Occasionally, a cell becomes discontented with the status quo. A disgruntled worker, it does not want anyone to tell it how to live, where to live, or how to reproduce. It loses its ability to grow and differentiate normally. This insurgent can clone copies of itself until there is a whole clan pursuing the dubious goal of anarchy. As the numbers increase, some of the anarchists hop into the bloodstream transport system and travel to other organ cities, where they cause further disruption. They infiltrate the tissue unions and cause strikes. If left unchecked, these dissidents can ultimately interrupt food supply and totally disrupt the order of the body. In a city with billions of residents, dissidents are not uncommon. The immune police force has many techniques for finding and arresting these troublemakers.

Carcinogenesis is the process by which a normal cell citizen is converted into a cancer anarchist. This force is thought to take the form of a mutation—a change to the genetic material in the nucleus of the cell. Such changes can be in the phosphate groups, the order of the bases, or in the three-dimensional structure of the DNA molecule. Many types of substances can cause mutations; environmental toxins, viruses, and radiation are some of the most common.

Mutation is a common event in the life of a cell, with several thousand errors introduced into our DNA each and every day. Cell citizens are bombarded every day with a wide variety of carcinogens. Some occur naturally, such as aflatoxin from the mold *Aspergillus flavus* and nitrosamines produced in the gastrointestinal tract. Others fall on us from the sky like the sun's ultraviolet rays or seep up at us from below like radon that's present in soil and rock gas. Numerous human-made chemicals are inhaled as cigarette smoke or industrial pollution. Asbestos fibers, polychlorinated biphenyls (PCBs), some insecticides, and vinyl chloride are other manufactured carcinogens.

Very often a mutation can be corrected by special enzymes that patrol the molecule, looking for mistakes. More than twenty different enzymes are dedicated to "spell-checking" your DNA words. Substances found in foods can increase the ability of these enzymes to seek and fix mutations. Also, many mutations occur in a genetic sequence that is crucial for survival, causing the cell to die before passing on the mutation. Only cells that survive these protective mechanisms have the potential to become cancerous.

Unfortunately, in spite of these defenses, carcinogenesis occasionally takes place. The process consists of three stages: initiation, promotion, and progression. Nutrition has an impact on all three.

Carcinogenesis: The Beginning of Cancer

A cell does not decide on its own to become an anarchist. It must first be initiated. If the mutation is not fixed and the cell divides and produces a copy of itself with the same mutation, then **initiation** is said to have occurred. Once initiation is completed, it cannot be undone.

The initiated cell is not a tumor cell. It can become a tumor cell only if it is acted upon by a promoter. In the majority of cases, this does not happen, and the cancerous cell dies without having spread its seditious manifesto. **Promoters** are substances that promote tumor growth in initiated cells. They have no effect on normal cells. Researchers believe that promoters do not work by changing the structure of DNA, since the effects of promotion are not permanent and can be reversed. The initiated cell must constantly be exposed to the promoter for tumor growth to occur. Promoters also alter the ability of cells to differentiate, producing cells that cannot mature. Some carcinogens are both initiators and promoters. They are called complete carcinogens. The female hormone estrogen is a cancer promoter in hormone-dependent cancers.

As the promoted cells multiply, they are very susceptible to another class of compounds called **progressive
agents**. Progressive agents cause the promoted cells to
reproduce. These agents cause further damage to the
chromosomes, resulting in a cell that loses the ability to
look and act like its neighbors. Progression, like initiation,
cannot be reversed.

Cancerous Tumors

Cancer comes from the Latin word for crab. Like a crab,
cancer attaches itself to tissues and organs and hangs on
obstinately. We often speak of cancer as if it were one specific disease, but this is not the case. Cancer is a group of
diseases that share a common characteristic: cells that
divide at a much greater rate than normal, causing masses
of tissue called tumors. Oncology (*oncos* means "tumor"
in Greek) is the study of neoplasia (*neo* = new, *plasia* =
growth). A new growth is called a **neoplasm**, another
word for tumor.

A tumor acts as a parasite, competing with normal tissues for food and energy. There are two types of tumors:
benign and malignant. Benign tumors grow slowly and
stay in one place. Malignant, or cancerous, tumors usually
grow rapidly and can spread to distant tissues by a process
called **metastasis**. Some of the malignant cells detach
from the tumor and travel to other parts of the body, usually through the blood or lymph vessels.

Malignant tumors are classified as either carcinomas or
sarcomas. Carcinomas develop from epithelial and endo-

thelial tissue such as the breast, skin, and lung and metastasize primarily to nearby tissues through the lymph system. Sarcomas arise from mesoderm tissue such as muscle, cartilage, and bone and spread primarily through the bloodstream. A tumor's histologic type is determined by the appearance and organization of the cells.

All tumors have two basic parts:

- The **parenchyma** is made up of the dividing and growing neoplastic cells; these cells determine the nature and type of the growth.
- The **stroma** is the supportive tissue made up of connective tissue and blood vessels. Without stromal support, a tumor would not survive. The stromal blood supply keeps the tumor supplied with food, and connective tissue provides a framework for the parenchyma.

Cancer treatments can target the parenchymal tissues, the stromal tissues, or both. Nutrition therapy also can affect both types of cancer tissues.

Most malignant tumors have grown from a single transformed cell (Figure 3.1). These clone cells are extremely susceptible to further mutation, producing strains of subclones. Subclones that lie low and do not call attention to themselves will not attract the interest of the immune system. These cells live longer and are able to multiply. Subclones that do provoke the immune system are promptly killed by white blood cells. Cells that have higher nutritional needs will not grow or spread as fast as those that thrive in a low-oxygen, low-energy environment. Like all life forms, the strongest survive.

Figure 3.1 Formation of a neoplasm

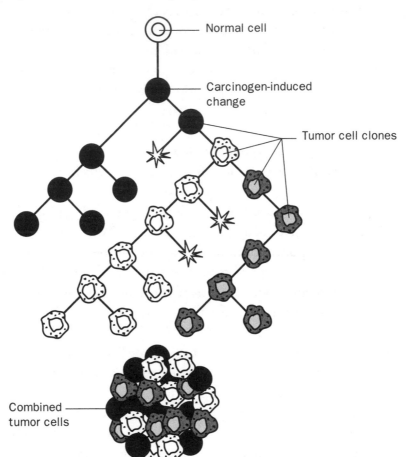

Normal cell

Carcinogen-induced change

Tumor cell clones

Combined tumor cells

Cells in cancerous tumors exhibit some important differences from their normal counterparts:

- Since the malignant cells are anarchists at heart, they grow in disorderly masses, uninhibited by contact with other cells. And unlike normal cells,

which like to be "tied" to a solid surface, malignant cells will flourish while floating free.
- Malignant cells never mature. They never differentiate into specialized cells. They are stuck in a sort of permanent adolescence, keeping their ability to reproduce but never differentiating into a particular type of cell with a normal job.
- Malignant cells are immortal. Normal cells differentiate and eventually die after a number of divisions. Some malignant cells have grown in culture dishes for decades.

Cancerous tumors are able to grow by infiltration, invasion, and destruction of the surrounding tissue.

Metastasis

For a clone cell from a tumor to spread, it must first find a way to get out of the surrounding normal tissue, push its way through the blood vessel wall, and then be able to reverse the process to set up housekeeping at a distant site (Figure 3.2). Your cells are held together with an adhesive molecule called **cadherin**. When cadherin loses its ability to stick to cells, they cannot hold on to each other. This is what allows cancer cells to detach from their neighbors so they can travel in the blood. Different cancers find different ways to interfere with cadherin production.

Cancer cells are also able to secrete factors that act like tiny machetes, so the escaping cells can cut their way through the basement membrane that surrounds and supports many types of cells.

Figure 3.2 Metastatic process

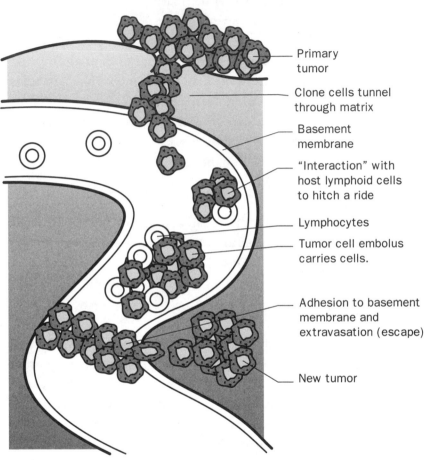

- Primary tumor
- Clone cells tunnel through matrix
- Basement membrane
- "Interaction" with host lymphoid cells to hitch a ride
- Lymphocytes
- Tumor cell embolus carries cells.
- Adhesion to basement membrane and extravasation (escape)
- New tumor

Angiogenesis and Tumor Growth

A cancer cell cannot spread if it does not have access to a blood vessel. This is where the process of angiogenesis comes in. Angiogenesis is the formation of new blood vessels. The body produces factors that stimulate angiogenesis and factors that prevent angiogenesis. In the adult body the factors that prevent angiogenesis are produced in larger amounts than those that stimulate it. The only exceptions to this are when injured tissue repairs itself, when the female body rebuilds uterine tissue lost during menstruation, and when the placenta is formed during pregnancy.

When cancer cells produce angiogenesis growth factors, they diffuse through the tissues where they ultimately reach the endothelial cells that form blood vessels. These factors then activate the production of enzymes that leave the endothelium and dissolve a hole in the basement membrane close to it. The endothelial cells sense the hole and grow toward it, producing a new blood vessel. As the vessel grows, it dissolves the tissue ahead of it, making room for further growth until the new vessel connects to an established blood supply. Finally blood flow begins, and the tiny tumor can get the nourishment to grow. Without new blood vessels a tumor could not grow larger than 2 millimeters (about one-tenth of an inch). These new blood vessels also offer a way for cells to escape and spread to other organs.

One of the most exciting new areas of cancer research involves the search for angiogenesis inhibitors that would choke off the blood supply to cancerous tumors. These drugs only recently have begun to be approved by the Federal Drug Administration. The first angiogenesis inhibitor (basic fibroblast growth factor, or bFGF) was isolated from shark cartilage, although studies in which shark cartilage was used to treat cancer patients have failed to see an effect. Green tea, ginseng, garlic, cumin, and licorice (the herb, not the candy!) are other natural sources of angiogenesis inhibitors.

Once the cell is circulating in the blood, it is very susceptible to the immune system army, particularly the natural killer (NK) cells, described in the next chapter. Metastasis can be slowed by keeping your NK cells fed and healthy.

Obesity and Tumor Growth

Recent research suggests that being obese may greatly increase the risk of developing cancer. Dr. Eugenia Calle and her group of researchers followed 900,000 men and women for sixteen years. They found that the men with the highest body mass index (BMI, a measure of obesity) had death rates from all cancers that were 52 percent higher than normal-weight men. Likewise, women with the highest BMI had cancer death rates 62 percent higher than their normal-weight counterparts.

This study also confirmed previous research that linked being overweight with the occurrence of cancers of the breast, colon and rectum, esophagus, gallbladder, kidney, and uterus. This means that being overweight or obese puts you at greater risk for developing cancer and then from dying from it. These researchers concluded that obesity may account for 20 percent of all cancer deaths in U.S. women and 14 percent in U.S. men. This means 90,000 cancer deaths could potentially be prevented through a change in diet and exercise.

Researchers believe that fat cells act like hormone pumps, dumping hormones and other growth factors into the bloodstream. The more fat a person carries and the less active they are, the more active the pumps. Constant exposure of cells to these growth factors causes cells to divide faster, and this leaves them open to developing mutations that cause cancer. When you have cancer, one of the best things you can do for yourself is to lose weight. The best way to lose weight is to follow a whole-foods diet that will provide the volume of food you need to satisfy your hunger while at the same time providing fewer calories. Exercise must also accompany any weight loss attempt.

Staging Tumors

To describe the extent of disease at the time of diagnosis, oncologists describe the tumor with a system of staging. Using this system helps your oncologist plan your treatment and compare different approaches. For solid tumors, the most frequently used system of staging is the **TNM classification** proposed by the American Joint Commission on Cancer:

- The *T* (for tumor) stands for the primary tumor or the place the cancer originated. The number next to it indicates the tumor's size or extent, with T1 being the smallest and T4 the largest; T0 means there is no evidence of a primary tumor, and Tis means cancer in situ, or cancer that is contained within the tissue.
- The *N* (for nodes) stands for the local or regional lymph nodes that drain the area of the primary tumor. The extent of node involvement goes from

N0 for no node involvement to N4 for extensive involvement.

- The *M* (for metastasis) denotes the absence (M0) or presence (M1) of metastasis, or spread.

Therefore, a TNM assignment of Tis N0 M0 indicates a cancer that has not invaded the local tissues (cancer in situ) and that has no lymph node involvement and no metastasis. A T3 N3 M1 assignment indicates a cancer with a large tumor that has grown extensively into the local tissue, a great deal of lymph node involvement, and metastasis. Not all types of cancer use this system of staging. Some use a modified version, some use a completely different system, and others use no system at all. Ask your oncologist to explain how your cancer is staged, and make sure you understand it.

4

The Body Strikes Back

Mutations are a common event in the life of a cell, and the body has developed mechanisms to prevent these mutations from doing damage. This chapter will introduce you to two of these mechanisms: the immune system and the antioxidant system. The immune system elements patrol the circulatory system and organs of the body on an antigen seek-and-destroy mission. The antioxidant system uses a group of substances to protect cells and tissues. This chapter will look at how these defense systems fight to free your body of cancer. It also identifies foods and nutrients necessary to support these systems.

When we think of the war on crime, we imagine police chasing robbers, muggers, and drug pushers. Often their efforts are not enough, and crime becomes an unavoidable complication of community life. But there is a place where such a war is fought and won on a daily basis—your body. In the microscopic world, the human body is surrounded by toxic gases, free radicals, damaging radiation, bacteria, viruses, parasites, and other sources of harm. The human body has two mechanisms for dealing with these situations: the immune system, which prevents the invasion of organisms, and the antioxidant system, which prevents damage from oxidation.

Recently science has recognized the critical role these systems play in cancer prevention. Often overlooked, however, are their ability to destroy cancers already present and the overwhelming importance of adequate nutrition to keep these systems running at peak efficiency.

The Immune System

The human body is gifted with the ability to keep itself free from disease-causing invaders. This immunity (from the Latin *immunitas*, meaning "freedom from disease") is achieved by the immune system, which is at once the smallest and the largest body system. Unlike the organ systems described Chapter 2, the immune system has no major organs of its own. It is composed of individual microscopic cells and molecules that have widespread access to every area of the body. The cells include lymphocytes (white blood cells), phagocytes, and natural killer (NK) cells, and the molecules include antibodies, complement, and interferon.

These immune elements see approaching objects in terms of black and white, as either bad or good. Scientists do not yet know how they do this or what criteria they use for classification. One theory is that the immune system somehow can tell the difference between the cell citizens, tissues, and proteins that belong to their body ("self") and all other proteins ("nonself").

The Antigen-Antibody Response

The nonself proteins are called **antigens**. Antigens may be peptides embedded in a living cell wall, fragments from a destroyed foreign cell, or stray proteins. A specific antigen stimulates the immune cells to manufacture a specific antibody. **Antibodies**, sometimes called immunoglobulins, are protein molecules that react only with their matching antigen, as a key fits into one specific lock. They can be located on the surface of a leukocyte as a receptor site or secreted as water-soluble antibodies that can travel far from the manufacturing cell. The antibody-antigen reaction sometimes renders the antigen harmless. Other times antibodies form a tasty coating on antigens, thereby attracting hungry scavenger cells.

Phagocytic Cells

The body's scavengers, called **phagocytes**, include neutrophils, monocytes, and other antigen-capturing white blood cells. They wander the highways and byways of the body, looking for something good to eat (phagocytize). When a neutrophil finds a nonself cell or protein, it simply eats it. The ingested particle is then killed with free radical bullets, described later in this chapter.

Monocytes patrol the blood. Some of them wander into the tissues where they transform into cells called **macrophages**. These cells are even more helpful to the immune soldiers than neutrophils. When a macrophage encounters an antigen, it swallows, digests, and displays a fragment of the antigen on its cell surface. The fragment serves as a sort of memento of what the macrophage has found in its travels, and it is used to make antibodies. Macrophages can also be summoned to infected areas by messages broadcast by lymphocytes, as described later in this chapter.

Phagocytes are also the cleanup crew after an immune battle. They eat the bodies of the dead lymphocytes and bacteria so that the corpses do not contribute to an infection.

Lymphocytes

Lymphocytes (white blood cells) are the infantrymen of the immune army. They come in two different types: **T cells** (or T lymphocytes), which are born in the thymus gland, and **B cells**, which are born in the bone marrow. Each T or B cell is programmed to recognize only one specific antibody by means of antigen receptor sites embedded on the cellular membrane. Each type of antigen has a corresponding B and T cell.

T lymphocytes are in charge of the cellular immunity division of the infantry. They are divided into two major types: helper-inducer T cells and cytotoxic–suppresser killer T cells. Helper T cells must be present to help B cells produce antibody. Cytotoxic T cells are regulatory cells.

The cytotoxic T cells are the most aggressive fighters in the army. They are able to detect spies: cells that appear normal on the outside but harbor a virus or mutated genes on the inside. Acting as both judge and executioner, the cytotoxic T cell decides who is abnormal and then kills the defective cell by riddling its cellular membrane with

holes or poisoning it with lethal toxins. T cells cannot recognize antibodies circulating in the blood. They will react
only to processed antibodies found by the macrophages
and monocytes of the phagocytic system.

The B cells control the humoral immunity division of
the infantry. They can manufacture numerous copies of
the antibodies they display on their membranes. These
water-soluble antibodies travel in the circulatory system,
quickly seeking out their victims.

Natural Killer Cells

In the fight against cancer, the most important cell is the
natural killer cell. Unlike killer T cells, NK cells do not
need to be activated by an antigen. This means that they
are able to attack and kill a wide variety of cells they have
never seen before. After activation by a molecule called
interleukin-2, NK cells can kill a wide variety of human
tumor cells that are not even recognized by the T and B
cells. Keeping these supersoldiers in optimal fighting condition is therefore necessary to beat cancer.

The Immune Response

Once a protein fragment has been displayed on the surface of an antigen-displaying cell, a corresponding antibody appears on both a B and a T cell. Then, when a T cell
with a specific antibody on its surface encounters an
antigen-displaying cell with the corresponding antigen on
its surface, it becomes activated. Activated T cells send an

alarm to other lymphocytes that an intruder has been discovered. They do this by secreting chemical messengers called **lymphokines**.

These specific lymphokines alert the corresponding B cells that the intruder has again been found. Some B cells respond to the alert by transforming into rapidly dividing plasma cells. Plasma cells are mobile antibody factories. Each plasma cell manufactures a specific antibody at the rate of ten million antibody molecules per hour.

Lymph Tissue

All of the immune cells travel in the bloodstream until they reach one of many secondary organs of the lymph system, such as the lymph nodes, spleen, or tonsils. There they congregate and mix with others, communicating with lymphokines and trading information on the types of antigens they have encountered in their travels. As many as one billion white blood cells can be found in as little as 1 gram of lymph tissue. When an antigen activates T and B cells, greatly increasing cell division, the increasing population of the lymph nodes can be felt by a physician. Swollen lymph nodes are a sign that an antigen has been found.

Nutrition and the Immune System

Like all armies, the immune system marches on its stomach. The adult body produces 126 billion new neutrophils every day. Normally about 25 billion are patrolling the blood, and another 2½ trillion are stationed in the bone marrow. Ten trillion lymphocytes are housed in the lymph tissues. This all adds up to a huge food bill. If these soldiers do not get the necessary nourishment, they will not be able to carry out their responsibilities or have energy for reproduction.

A lack of many trace minerals and vitamins will decrease the activity of these soldiers. The following list summarizes how some of these shortages affect the immune system:

- *Zinc*—a shortage causes a decrease in T killer cell and NK cell activity.
- *Iron*—a deficiency reduces NK cell cytotoxicity, phagocytosis, and the killing capacity of neutrophils.
- *Copper*—a lack reduces the population of T cells and depresses the immune system.
- *Selenium*—a deficiency decreases antibody production.
- *Selenium and vitamin E*—a shortage of these two synergistic nutrients will decrease the cytotoxic function of NK cells.
- *Pyridoxine*—a lack of this B vitamin reduces antibody production and decreases the ability of lymphocytes to function.

The following vitamins also affect the immune system:

- *Vitamin C*—an antioxidant nutrient that protects the watery areas of the cell from the "friendly fire"

of cancer treatment. As an antihistamine, it detoxifies histamine, which can depress the immune
system.
- *Vitamin E*—an antioxidant nutrient that protects
  the lipid components of cells, including the cell
  membrane and the membranes surrounding various
  organelles. It works synergistically with selenium.
- *Vitamin A*—a fat-soluble vitamin that inhibits the
  growth and development of cancer. A deficiency
  decreases the number of plasma cells producing
  antibody.

But strong warriors are only part of the story. The
immune fighters must also be properly armed and able to
transmit and receive communications. The molecules
needed for this are formed from protein, and so a lack of
this macronutrient will decrease the amount of antibody
bombs the army can produce and reduce the number of
messages exchanged.

Protective elements also are important. Antioxidant
nutrients and phytochemicals are needed to enhance these
systems and protect healthy cells from treatment-induced
free radicals (described in the next section).

Fats such as fish and flaxseed oil inhibit the ability of
cancer cells to spread by hindering attachment. The types
of dietary fatty acids influence the composition and fluid-
ity of macrophage membranes, impairing their ability to
kill tumor cells. When animals are fed diets high in polyunsaturated or saturated fats, the cytotoxic abilities of
macrophages decrease.

Free Radicals and Oxidation

One of the most common causes of cellular injury and death is damage from free radicals. These dangerous molecules can be caused by radiation and chemical injury, cellular aging, microbial killing by phagocytic cells, inflammatory damage, and tumor destruction by macrophages.

When a molecule either steals an electron from another molecule or adds an oxygen molecule to it, the process is called oxidation. The result can be a free radical. This is a molecule that has a single unpaired electron in its outer orbit. Electrons have a compulsion to travel in pairs, and molecules that lack an electron will go to almost any length to acquire a new partner. They will react with lipids, proteins, or carbohydrates. Particularly vulnerable are the components of the cellular membrane and DNA. The most dangerous free radicals are the ones that contain oxygen. Because they react so easily with molecules, they are called reactive oxygen species (ROS). An example of oxidation is the browning of cut fruit such as an apple. When an apple is sliced, oxygen from the air reacts with the cells on the surface and the damage is visible as a brown discoloration. Once this reaction occurs, the molecule is no longer reactive. However, the molecule it got the electron from is now reactive and looking for another electron, starting a chain reaction of damage that can punch holes in cellular membranes and cause mutations in your genetic material.

The body has two main mechanisms for ridding itself of free radicals:

- It can obtain **antioxidants** (agents that protect against electron loss to free radicals), manufacturing them inside the body or obtaining them from the diet.
- The body also has a system of enzymes to neutralize the free radicals generated as a result of normal metabolism.

Antioxidant Nutrients

The most commonly recognized antioxidant nutrients are beta-carotene (a precursor to vitamin A), vitamins C and E, coenzyme Q10, and selenium. They are, however, only the tip of the iceberg. Beta-carotene is just one of many carotenoids with antioxidant properties, not the most powerful. Other powerful carotenes include alpha-carotene, lycopene, lutein, and cryptoxanthin. Never take more than 10,000 IU of beta-carotene; doing so can decrease serum levels of these carotenes.

Flavonoids, like carotenoids, are a large family of pigments. Those with antioxidant activity include rutin, quercetin, myricetin, and the citrus flavones. Other pigments that neutralize free radicals are the proanthocyanidins, tannins, and anthocyanins.

Antioxidant Enzymes

Enzymes needed by the human body are manufactured using DNA templates. Although certain vitamins, minerals, and phytochemicals (bioactive plant chemicals) act as free radical quenchers, the body's primary defense against free radicals is its enzyme systems. These systems produce the weapons with which the immune army attacks invaders and insurgents. The major enzymes used by the body are glutathione peroxidase, superoxide dismutase, and catalase.

Glutathione Peroxidase

Glutathione peroxidase is used primarily by the cells of the liver, lungs, heart, and blood to deactivate reactive oxygen species before they can cause injury. It inactivates the hydrogen peroxide free radical and scavenges lipid peroxides, the free radicals formed when oxygen radicals attack the unsaturated fatty acids in the cell membrane. As a result, the membrane loses two essential fatty acids: arachidonic acid and linoleic acid. This loss increases the permeability of the membrane, leading to an imbalance of minerals, including calcium, magnesium, sodium, and potassium.

Selenium is a part or cofactor of this enzyme, and vitamins C and E enhance its effects. In fact, some studies suggest that combining selenium and vitamin E with glutathione is more effective for cancer prevention than using either alone. Glutathione and the amino acid cystine can increase levels of glutathione peroxidase. Glutathione is found in many foods.

Superoxide Dismutase and Catalase

Cells use superoxide dismutase (SOD) to prevent damage by the superoxide free radical. If not quenched, the superoxide free radical degenerates into the lethal hydroxyl radical. SOD prevents this by demoting the superoxide radical to the less toxic hydrogen peroxide. The hydroxyl radical is dangerous because it can steal electrons from virtually any organic molecule in the immediate area. When SOD works in the mitochondria, it requires manganese. When used in the cytoplasm, it requires copper and zinc.

Catalase is the enzyme that completes the reaction started by SOD. It does so by reducing the hydrogen peroxide radical to oxygen and water. Catalase performs its work in the blood and the peroxisomes (enzyme-containing organelles) of cells. It requires the mineral iron as a cofactor.

The immune system is like an army with a vast contingent of soldiers, including lymphocytes, phagocytes, macrophages, and natural killer cells. These cells either kill invaders directly or secrete substances that kill them indirectly. Proper nutrition is necessary to feed the immune cells and provide the antioxidants necessary to protect healthy cells from cancer treatment. Like all armies, the immune army must be well fed in order to fight. The nutrients it needs can sometimes be supplemented. But the supplementation in turn must be supplemented by healthy amounts of fruits, vegetables, whole grains, and other whole foods. This will ensure that you get all of the nutrients, known and unknown, that your immune army needs.

5

Carbohydrates and Cancer

Carbohydrates are sugar chains of varying lengths. They are made by plants as a way of storing energy from the sun. The body uses them to supply energy for heat and mechanical work, spare protein and fats, feed the healthy colonic bacteria, and provide indigestible fiber for colon health. In the human diet, carbohydrates provide most of the energy for the cell citizens. They are carried in the blood as glucose and regulated by the hormone insulin. A high blood sugar level feeds cancer tumors. Whole foods rich in complex carbohydrates prevent quick rises in blood glucose that may feed cancerous cells. They are also sources of other cancer-fighting vitamins, minerals, and phytochemicals. This chapter explores the effect of carbohydrates on blood sugar and cancer.

Types of Carbohydrates

Without a doubt, our favorite macronutrient is the carbohydrate. It fills the stomach and calms the mind as no other nutrient can. There are three general types of carbohydrates: simple, digestible, and indigestible.

Monosaccharides

Simple carbohydrates, or sugars, are easily recognized in foods because of their sweet taste. The basic unit of the carbohydrate is the monosaccharide (*mono* = one, *saccharide* = sugar), and the main carbohydrate of the body is **glucose** (blood sugar). Other monosaccharides include **fructose** (the main sugar in fruit) and **galactose** (which, together with glucose, forms lactose, or milk sugar).

Monosaccharides are classified by how many carbon atoms they have. Fructose, glucose, and galactose are all made of six carbons in a ring. Actually these simple sugars are all composed of the same elements: six carbon, twelve oxygen, and twelve hydrogen atoms arranged in a ring. They are called **hexoses** (*hex* = six, *ose* = sugar). The molecular formula is written as $C_6H_{12}O_6$.

The purpose of eating carbohydrates and most fats is to provide the body with glucose. Glucose provides the fuel for almost all cells and is the only form in which sugar can be transported in the bloodstream. For example, your central nervous system uses nine tablespoons of glucose each day, and your red blood cells use three tablespoons.

Disaccharides

Two joined monosaccharides form a disaccharide (*di* = two). Three disaccharides are found in the food you eat. **Sucrose** is the disaccharide you are probably most familiar with, since it is the sole component of refined white sugar. It is made up of one molecule of glucose joined to one molecule of fructose. **Lactose** is found only in milk and enhances the absorption of its calcium. Lactose is composed of one glucose molecule and one galactose molecule. **Maltose** is composed of two glucose molecules. It is found only in germinating cereals and is used to make malt beverages. Barley malt syrup is a tasty alternative to refined sugar.

The enzymes **sucrase** and **lactase** are necessary to break apart sucrose and lactose into their component monosaccharides. These two sugars lie on top of the microvilli of the small intestine. Anything that injures the microvilli, such as radiation and chemotherapy, will affect the body's ability to digest and absorb these sugars. This results in the sucrose or lactose reaching the colon undigested, where it attracts water, resulting in diarrhea. In addition, bacteria in the colon ferment the sugar to produce flatulence and cramping.

Millions of people in the United States have lost the ability to digest lactose, a condition called lactose intolerance. This may be a temporary condition during cancer treatment. Anytime you have severe diarrhea, it may indicate that the villi are damaged and that you should avoid lactose-containing foods until they have healed.

Polysaccharides

Chains of many simple sugars are called polysaccharides (*poly* = many) or starches. Starches come in two types: amylose and amylopectin. **Amylose** is made of several hundred glucose units arranged in a straight, unbranched chain. **Amylopectin** is made of several thousand glucose units arranged in highly branched chains.

The shape of each starch molecule gives you a clue as to how it affects the body. Amylose, being a single chain, has only two ends for enzymes to attack. Digestion of this starch is going to be slow; the end products will enter the blood slowly and raise blood glucose levels slowly. Amylose can be considered a time-release form of energy. The many chains of amylopectin offer the enzymes more places to snap off glucose and maltose molecules. Digestion is going to be quicker, and glucose will enter the bloodstream and raise glucose levels quickly.

Whereas plants store carbohydrates in the form of starch, animals store carbohydrates in a large, branched molecule called **glycogen**. It is the most available form of glucose. About three-quarters of a pound of glycogen is stored in the liver and muscles—enough to keep the body fueled for half a day. If more carbohydrates are eaten than are needed for immediate use, the remainder are stored as glycogen. When the glycogen capacity of the liver and muscle is filled, the rest of the carbohydrates are converted to fat and stored in adipose tissues.

Cellulose is the most abundant organic (carbon-containing) substance on earth. It forms the structural framework of almost all plants, giving them shape. The glucose units that compose cellulose have a type of bond that resists breakdown by human enzymes. This means that the cellulose from fruits, vegetables, legumes, and grains enters the colon without being digested. Cellulose is the component of fiber that absorbs and holds water, increasing the bulk and softness of the feces.

Fiber

We're told these days that we need fiber (roughage or bulk) for a well-functioning digestive tract and to lower risk factors for cancer, heart disease, hypertension, and diabetes. However, no one definition for fiber is totally accepted, nor is it well known how fiber prevents these diseases. A good definition of fiber is a group of carbohydrates or substances made from carbohydrates that show three properties: (1) they resist digestion by human enzymes; (2) they are able to reach the colon in much the same form in which they were eaten; and (3) they have some effect on gastrointestinal function.

Fiber is composed of cellulose, hemicellulose, pectin, algal substances, gums, and mucilages. **Crude fiber** is a scientific measurement of the cellulose and lignin in a food that is treated with acid and alkali. Estimates of crude fiber are often found in food tables. **Dietary fiber** includes two to five times more substances than crude fiber. It includes cellulose, lignin, hemicelluloses, gums, pectin, and other fibers.

Fiber can be divided into two main subclasses. These are commonly called soluble and insoluble.

Soluble fiber. As its name suggests, soluble fiber is able to dissolve in the watery contents of the digestive tract, where it is thickened into a gel-like consistency. It is easily fermented by the "friendly" bacteria that grow in the colon and is able to affect the entire body.

Soluble fiber reaches the colon without being digested. There it is fermented by bacteria to produce gases (carbon dioxide, hydrogen, and methane); lactic acid; and short-chain fatty acids, mainly acetate, propionate, and butyrate. These fermentation products then interact with the cells of the digestive tract or are absorbed into the bloodstream. Short-chain fatty acids can travel to the liver, where they reduce cholesterol production and influence the metabolism of glucose and fats.

A diet high in soluble fiber is associated with a lower serum cholesterol, lower insulin levels in the blood, and an increased feeling of fullness. Soluble fiber also slows the rate at which food leaves the stomach. Pectin, gums, mucilages, and algal substances are examples of soluble fiber.

Insoluble fiber. The other category of fiber, insoluble fiber, is not appetizing to the colonic bacteria and leaves the body in much the same form as it entered. Insoluble fiber has a local effect on the digestive tract, increasing the size and weight of feces through water absorption. This increases the frequency of bowel movements, stimulates peristaltic movement, and reduces the time it takes for food to travel through the digestive system. A diet rich in insoluble fiber is associated with a decreased risk of colon and rectal cancer, decreased constipation, and a reduction in blood pressure.

Cellulose, hemicellulose, and lignin are insoluble fibers. Cellulose, mentioned earlier, is found in fruit and vegetable pulp, skin, stems, and leaves and in the outer covering of nuts, seeds, and grains. **Hemicellulose** is a polysaccharide made from hexoses, pentoses, and acid forms of hexoses and pentoses, as well as glucose units. It is found along with cellulose. **Lignin** is a fiber that is not a carbohydrate, although it is found in the cell walls of plants. Sources include wheat bran and woody portions of fruits and vegetables. Lignin is associated with a lower incidence of breast and ovarian cancers.

Alcohol

When yeast ferments the glucose in sugar, fruits, or cereal grains, ethanol (a type of alcohol) is produced. Chemically, **ethanol** is a small, water-soluble molecule that is absorbed very easily. It is metabolized and detoxified in the liver.

Alcohol is a double-edged sword. In some people it causes addiction, and in others it is health promoting. Alcohol can interact with other drugs and alter their effectiveness, so it is very important to tell your doctor how much alcohol you consume each day. Alcohol also puts additional stress on the liver at a time when this important organ needs support. We recommend that you avoid all alcohol during your cancer treatment. If you would like to continue receiving the health benefits of wine, substitute purple grape juice.

Function of Carbohydrates

The body needs a constant supply of carbohydrates in the form of glucose for all metabolic reactions. The energy needs of the body take precedence over all other needs. The main function of carbohydrates is to provide a source of energy. Each gram of carbohydrate provides approximately 4 kilocalories (usually used in the shortened form *calorie*) of energy. This is true of both sugars and starches.

Carbohydrates have a protein-sparing effect. This means that if not enough carbohydrates are consumed, the body will then turn to protein as an energy source. For amino acids to be absorbed and used properly, they must be consumed with carbohydrates. Therefore, one way to increase the amount of protein available for new tissue synthesis is to consume a diet high in carbohydrates.

Carbohydrates are also necessary for normal fat metabolism. If not enough carbohydrates are consumed, the body can also turn to fat for energy. This is the theory behind dieting for weight loss. But the conversion of fat to glucose can go only so fast, and soon the process is starting faster than it can finish. Intermediate products called **ketones** build up and can cause acidosis (too much acid in the blood). Sodium combines with these acids, and they are excreted as sodium salts in urine. This high concentration of sodium in the urine then pulls water into the urine, leading to dehydration and a loss of sodium. The initial weight loss from a very low-calorie diet is due to water loss, and the accompanying bad breath is due to the excretion of ketones by the lungs.

Glucose is the sole energy source for the brain. Any lack of glucose, or of oxygen to burn the glucose, results in permanent brain damage. Carbohydrates and their products are also precursors of nucleic acids, connective tissue matrix, and galactosides of nerve tissue.

Sugar Red Flags

Sugars often appear on food labels and ingredient lists under different names. Beware when you see these terms:

Fructose	Maltose
Glucose	Barley malt
High-fructose corn syrup	Brown rice syrup
Sucrose	Honey
Corn syrup	Molasses
Lactose	Fruit juice
Milk sugar	Naturally sweetened
Dextrose	Fruit juice concentrate

In addition, whole foods that are good sources of carbohydrates are also good sources of protein, minerals, and the B vitamins necessary for carbohydrate metabolism.

Metabolism of Carbohydrates

Carbohydrates must be broken down into their component monosaccharides before they can be absorbed. The glucose absorbed through the intestine immediately goes into the portal vein, which transports it to the liver and eventually the bloodstream. As a meal is digested, the amount of blood glucose rises. In response to the glucose in the blood, the pancreas secretes a hormone called **insulin** into the blood. This results in glucose and insulin reaching the hungry cell at the same time.

Glucose cannot enter a cell without insulin. Insulin is like a key that turns the insulin receptor lock, opening a door in the cell membrane that allows glucose to enter via a glucose transport unit (GLUT). When not enough insulin is secreted, the cells can be surrounded by glucose but unable to use it, since all their doors are locked. This is the dilemma in diabetes, where some of the excess sugar is excreted in the urine.

When the glucose enters a cell, it has several options. If the cell is hungry, the glucose is used immediately to make energy. If the cell is not hungry, the glucose is changed by muscle and liver cells into glycogen for temporary storage. If the storage room for glycogen is filled up, the remaining glucose is changed into fat and stored in regular cells or in the adipose (fat storage) cells.

The next time cells get hungry and no glucose is available from a meal, the glycogen stored in the muscles and liver is changed back into glucose and fed to the cells. When the glycogen is used up, fat is used to make glucose. This stimulates the appetite, causing you to eat more and make more glucose available. The process of making new glucose is called **gluconeogenesis** (*gluco* = sugar, *neo* = new, *genesis* = to make).

Sometimes when insulin and glucose meet a hungry cell, they find that insulin does not unlock the receptor site or glucose is unable to enter through the open door because no GLUTs are available. The cell is then said to be resistant to the effects of insulin, or insulin resistant.

Fructose also is absorbed into the portal system. Its atoms are rearranged to form glucose in the liver. The liver then releases the glucose when it deems fit. No other organ can change fructose into glucose so no other organ can use fructose. Fructose also does not stimulate insulin release and so does not directly raise blood sugar. As a result fructose escapes the tight control the body has on glucose metabolism. The end result is that fructose does not dampen the appetite and it can lead to overeating. It also raises plasma triglycerides (fats).

Carbohydrates and Cancer

Cancer cells in a tumor like to eat glucose and will alter the metabolism of the body to get more of it. They do this by increasing glucose formation in the liver from amino acids, which leads to a loss of muscle tissue from the skeleton and internal organs. Insulin resistance is increased so that glucose is less able to enter healthy cells. All of this results in hyperglycemia, or high blood sugar levels.

One of the purposes of nutrition therapy for cancer is to deny the growing tumor glucose while providing enough to feed the brain and to form red blood cells. This can be done in a crude way by keeping the blood sugar levels even. One way to do this is to eat foods that have a low glycemic index or low glycemic load.

The Glycemic Index and Glycemic Load

The **glycemic index (GI)** is a measure of how fast the carbohydrates in a food increase blood sugar levels.

Healthy volunteers are given 50 grams of carbohydrates from a variety of carbohydrate-rich foods, and their blood sugar levels are measured two hours later. Foods are assigned a number, with 100 being pure glucose. A high-GI carbohydrate causes a spike in blood glucose levels. Foods with a GI of 70 or more are considered high-GI foods. Foods with a GI of 55 or less are considered low-GI foods. The carbohydrates in a low-GI food do not cause a large spike.

The first attempts to establish GI charts were crude because they were cobbled together from a variety of different studies performed in a number of different of labs that often used different methods of testing. But today researchers have refined and standardized the glycemic index. Unfortunately many of the GI listings we see around are not taken from the more recent studies but from the older outdated lists. Probably the most accurate are those of Sydney University's Glycemic Index Research Service.

The major problem with the glycemic index is that it does not take into consideration how much carbohydrate is present in a serving of food. Therefore, a carrot is often listed as having a high GI. This is true, but it is also true that a serving of carrots has very little of that high-GI carbohydrate, and what is there is accompanied by a lot of fiber which slows glucose absorption. Eating carrots will not increase blood glucose levels.

A better indicator of the effect of a particular food on blood sugar levels is the **glycemic load (GL)**, the amount of carbohydrate multiplied by its GI. This measure was developed to make the results of the GI much more consumer-friendly and accurate.

Glycemicindex.com makes these suggestions for eating a low GI/GL diet:

- Use breakfast cereals based on oats, barley, and bran.
- Use breads with whole grains, stone-ground flour, and sourdough.
- Reduce the amount of potatoes you eat.
- Enjoy all other types of fruit and vegetables.
- Use basmati, Doongara, or Japanese Koshihikari rice.
- Enjoy pasta, noodles, and quinoa.
- Eat plenty of salad vegetables with a vinaigrette dressing.

Problems with the GI/GL

Neither the GI nor the GL has been embraced enthusiastically by the nutrition community. While researchers have found that both can help control blood sugar levels, nutritionists and dietitians who work with patients are less enthused. The problem is that the GI and GL can be difficult to use in the real world because too many factors can vary.

Both measure each food separately, yet we do not eat food this way; we eat combinations of foods in a meal. It is possible to calculate the GI/GL of a mixed meal, but it is difficult and the results vary. The GI/GL does not take other components of the meal, such as fiber and fat, into consideration. Both can decrease the time it takes for food to leave the stomach so it is absorbed slowly and the glucose released from it increases slowly. The size of the food particle, length of cooking time, and extent of processing also affect how much a food increases glucose levels. Finally the response to a food varies from person to person and from day to day.

Low-Carbohydrate Diets

Another way to decrease serum glucose levels is to follow a low-carbohydrate diet. This type of diet has been around since the 1800s and periodically goes in and out of favor. A low-carb diet is usually one that gets 40 percent of its calories from carbohydrates. The other 60 percent of calories is then divided equally between protein and fat.

Low-carb diets suffer from the same problem as both glycemic measures: they are difficult to follow even when you are healthy because food choices are so limited. When you are not feeling well, it may be impossible. Many people who think they are on a low-carb diet actually are not. Studies done on dieters show that people following low-carb diets eat fewer calories. This can also be a problem if you are already not consuming enough energy to prevent weight loss. Finally, low-carb diets often do not contain foods rich in the antioxidants, vitamins, and minerals you need to fight cancer.

We have included a "lower" carb diet in Part II for those who want to decrease their carbohydrate intake this way. It contains more carbohydrates than most low-carb diets to provide more variety.

A Third Option

There is an easier and better way to control your blood glucose levels: the whole-foods diet. Foods rich in whole grains, fruits, vegetables, and fiber are low glycemic too. There are no charts to figure out, and unlike the low-carb diet, a bounty of food choices are available. Avoid foods that are overly processed and/or refined, high in added sugar, and made with refined flour. Instead, choose foods that are naturally sweet, such as fruit. Other suggestions include:

- Avoid eating or drinking anything that tastes sweet on an empty stomach. This includes sweet-tasting fruit and vegetable juices, fruit, soda, sweetened refined cereals, honey, or any liquid sweetened with any form of sugar.
- Always eat a balanced meal with mixed foods. A meal rich in complex carbohydrates and fiber will slow the release of food from the stomach, thereby slowing the release of glucose from the meal.
- Eat sweet whole foods such as fruit only with meals. Drink diluted or low-sugar fruit and vegetable juices only with fat-containing meals.
- Learn carbohydrate counting. This is a technique used by many diabetics to control the carbohydrate content of their diets. It is much easier to learn than other methods of keeping track of carbs.

A diet in which most of the calories came from unrefined carbohydrates is also rich in many other nutrients that can inhibit the growth of cancer cells.

6

Lipids, Fats, and Cancer

Fats are made by animals as a way of storing energy obtained from plants. This energy can be in the guise of preformed fat, carbohydrate, or protein. All fats contain the same number of calories, but not all fats are created equal. This chapter will help you distinguish between healthy fats and those that may promote cancer growth and development.

The word *fat* gets a lot of bad press. Fat is not a single homogeneous group. Some fats are good, and some are bad. Sometimes it is not the type of fats eaten that causes a problem, but the amount eaten. Too much fat in the diet is linked with increased tumor growth. This may be the result of fats stimulating the multiplication and spread of cancer cells, inhibiting the immune system, or both. Natural killer cell activity is increased when fat intake is decreased to 25 percent of calories from fat. For those with hormone-dependent cancers such as breast cancer, a very low-fat diet (less than 20 percent of calories from fat) may slow the spread of cancer cells. On the other hand, some types of fat decrease the inflammation that can cause cachexia—cancer-induced weight loss. Cancer also inter-feres with the normal process of fat storage, making it less efficient. This is a concern when weight loss is a problem.

The words *fats*, *oils*, and *lipids* are used interchangeably for the same nutrient. Technically fats and oils (which are liquid fats) are part of a group of substances called **lipids**. In a general sense, lipids are organic (carbon-containing) substances that will not dissolve in water. Other terms that add to the confusion are *saturated fats*, *polyunsaturated fats*, *omega-3 fats*, *monounsaturates*, *essential fatty acids*, *nonessential fatty acids*, *fish oil*, *olive oil*, *cholesterol*, *MCT*, *EPO*, *EPA*, *DHA*, *GLA*, and *lecithin*. All of these "fat" terms are used freely in conversation, but few people really under-stand what they are or what they do. To appreciate the important role lipids play in cancer therapy, a little lesson in biochemistry is in order.

Fatty Acids

The basic building block of lipids is the fatty acid. Fatty acids are composed of carbon atoms arranged in a chain. At one end of the chain is a methyl group (CH_3), and at the other end is the carboxyl group (COOH) (Figure 6.1). Two smaller fatty acids can be joined together to produce a longer fatty acid by connecting the methyl end of one with the carboxyl group of the other.

The fatty acids that are the building blocks of lipids can be classified according to the degree of saturation, loca-tion of the first double bond, and length of the carbon chain.

Figure 6.1 Composition of a fatty acid

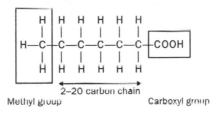

2–20 carbon chain

Methyl group   Carboxyl group

Saturated and Unsaturated Fatty Acids

Each carbon atom in the carbon chain of a fatty acid has sites for two hydrogen atoms. When the carbon chain of a fatty acid has all the hydrogen atoms it can hold, it is said to be **saturated**. The chain of a saturated fatty acid is straight, making it easy for saturated fat molecules to be packed tightly together (Figure 6.2). This results in a solid fat at room temperature. Saturated fatty acids are very stable and do not go rancid easily. However, many saturated fats increase cholesterol production and blood cholesterol levels. Butter is a natural fat that is high in saturated fatty acids.

Figure 6.2 Saturated fatty acid

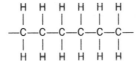

When two hydrogen atoms are removed from two adjacent carbon atoms, the carbon atoms use the available sites to add another bond between them, making it a double bond. A fatty acid with one double bond is said to be a **monounsaturated fatty acid** (*mono* = one) (Figure 6.3). The double bond also causes a kink in the chain. This makes it difficult to stack the chains, just as it is difficult to stack folded chairs on top of one that is partially open. The chains, like the folded chairs, fall around each other; as a result, the fat is a liquid. The greater the percentage of monounsaturated fatty acids in a fat, the more fluid it becomes.

Figure 6.3 Monounsaturated fatty acid

$$
\begin{array}{cccccc}
& H & H & & H & H \\
& | & | & & | & | \\
-C & -C & -C & =C & -C & -C- \\
| & | & | & | & | & | \\
H & H & H & H & H & H
\end{array}
$$

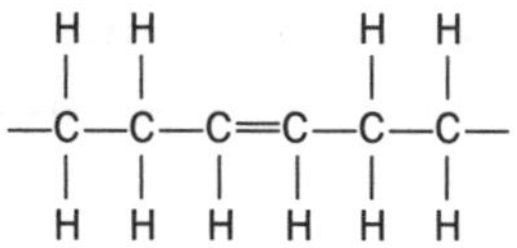

In longer carbon chains, more than one double bond may be formed. These fatty acids are called **polyunsaturated fatty acids** (*poly* = many) (Figure 6.4). Because polyunsaturated fatty acids have two or more double bond "kinks," fats that contain a high percentage of polyunsaturates are liquid at room temperature. Polyunsaturates keep the membranes of cells fluid and pliable.

Figure 6.4 Polyunsaturated fatty acid

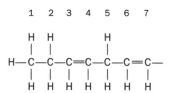

The double bonds in polyunsaturated fatty acids are vulnerable to attack from oxygen in the air. The addition of oxygen (oxidation) causes changes in flavor and odor which are commonly called rancidity. Rancid oils can be toxic in large doses. To prevent oxidation in some polyunsaturated fatty acids, hydrogen is added to the double-bonded carbons, breaking the additional bond and making the fatty acid more stable. This is called **hydrogenation** (Figure 6.5).

Figure 6.5 Hydrogenation

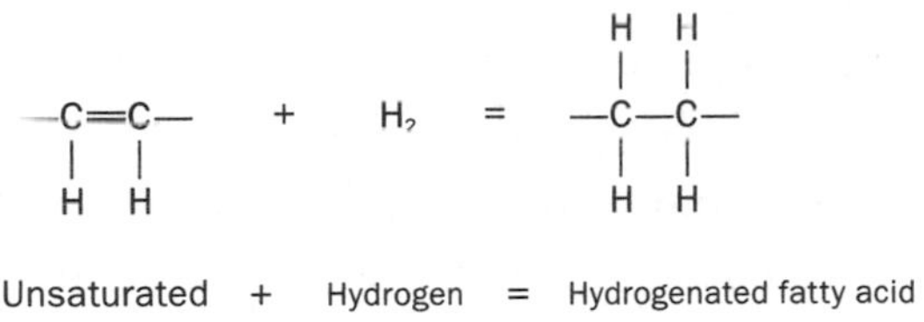

$$
-C{=}C- \quad + \quad H_2 \quad = \quad -\overset{\displaystyle H}{\underset{\displaystyle H}{C}}-\overset{\displaystyle H}{\underset{\displaystyle H}{C}}-
$$

Unsaturated + Hydrogen = Hydrogenated fatty acid

Hydrogenated oils are solid at room temperature. The greater the degree of saturation, the more solid a fat becomes. The lower the saturation, the more liquid it becomes. Tub margarines have a lower degree of saturation than those that come in cubes. When fatty acids are hydrogenated, they increase the saturation of fats. A high intake of saturated fats is a risk factor for many diseases.

Omega Number and Length

Another way of classifying fatty acids is by the location of the first double bond. This location is found by counting from the methyl end of the molecule. For example, in the preceding figure of a polyunsaturated fatty acid, the first double bond is found on the third carbon. Therefore, its omega number is 3. Oils rich in omega-3 fatty acids (in particular, fish oil) are often in the news these days.

Three important omega-3 fatty acids are eicosapentaenoic acid (EPA), docosahexaenoic acid (DHA), and linolenic acid. Both EPA and DHA can be manufactured by the body from linolenic acid, but sometimes it may not produce all that it needs. EPA and DHA are found in fish oil.

The omega-3 fats are also precursors for prostaglandins, messenger molecules that enable the endothelial cells to "talk" to local tissues. The omega-3 fatty acids produce series 1 and 3 prostaglandins, which send "good" messages that reduce inflammation, prevent blood clotting by decreasing platelet stickiness, and tell your arteries to relax.

The omega-6 fatty acids also have unique properties. They include linoleic acid; arachidonic acid, which is manufactured from linoleic acid; and gamma linolenic acid (GLA). The omega-6 fatty acids are precursors to the series 2 prostaglandins (PGE_2), which promote inflammation and encourage blood clotting and cellular growth. Series 2 prostaglandins reduce the ability of macrophages and natural killer cells to kill cancer cells and tumors.

The production of PGE_2, requires the same enzymes as the production of PGE_1 and PGE_3, which means that the omega-3 fatty acids oppose the effects of the omega-6 fatty acids. When you eat a diet rich in arachidonic acid your body will produce more PGE_2, and your body will suffer the effects. When you eat a diet rich in the omega-

3 fatty acids your body will produce more PGE_1 and PGE_3, and your body will benefit.

Unfortunately, the typical Western diet that is high in meat and animal products is high in omega-6 fatty acids and low in omega-3 fatty acids. There needs to be a balance between the two.

Gamma linoleic acid is the good omega-6 fatty acid. It is not turned into arachidonic acid, as linoleic acid is. GLA is manufactured as a result of the first step toward the production of another series of helpful prostaglandins. Not everyone manufactures enough GLA; those who do not can benefit from supplements. Good sources of GLA are evening primrose oil and borage tree oil. However, our diets tend to contain too many omega-6 fatty acids and too few omega-3 fatty acids. If we supplement both types, we will not get the full benefit of the omega-3s.

Chain Length

Fatty acids are also described by the length of their carbon chain. Formic acid (released in bee stings and ant bites) has only one carbon atom. Acetic acid (vinegar) has two carbon atoms. Since these fatty acids are so short, they are soluble in water, making them act more like water soluble acids. The fatty acids found in food range from four carbons (butyric acid) to twenty-four (found in fish oils).

Within this range, fatty acids are described as having short, medium, or long chains:

- Short-chain fatty acids contain two to six carbon atoms. They are found in butter and milk.

- Medium-chain fatty acids contain eight to twelve carbon atoms. These are very easy to absorb and are available at pharmacies as medium-chain triglycerides (MCTs). Coconut milk is very rich in MCTs.
- Long-chain fatty acids contain sixteen or more carbon atoms.

Medium-chain triglycerides. Medium-chain triglycerides need very little lipase and no bile to be digested. Unlike the long-chain fatty acids, they do not need to be reassembled into triglycerides after absorption. They dissolve easily into the bloodstream and are carried to the liver via the portal vein. Because they bypass the slow-moving lymph system, MCTs are absorbed as quickly as glucose. They are an excellent source of energy for cancer patients who have damaged intestinal villi due to malnutrition, radiation, or chemotherapy or those who lack sufficient pancreatic enzymes or bile acids.

Pure MCT can be purchased in pharmacies without a prescription as a pure oil and with a prescription as an ingredient in some medical foods. MCT oil is not very palatable and must be mixed with other foods. Coconut milk is a good source of palatable MCTs.

MCTs have not been shown to be useful for weight loss, although they are sometimes recommended for this. However, MCTs do appear to have some antitumor effect which may be useful in your diet. When used for malabsorption problems, the typical dose is 1 tablespoon of MCT oil up to three times a day. One tablespoon is equal to 15 grams of MCTs. Do not exceed this dose; when taken all at once, doses of more than 80 grams (or 5 tablespoons) can cause strong cramping in the intestines.

Applying the Classifications: An Example

Let's see how we would classify the molecule in Figure 6.6. We know it is a fatty acid because it follows the formula of a methyl group at one end, a carboxyl group at the other, and two to twenty carbons in between. It has three double bonds, so it is a polyunsaturated fatty acid. With eighteen carbon atoms, it is a long-chain fatty acid. Double bonds are at carbon numbers 3, 6, and 9, so its omega number is 3.

Figure 6.6 Linolenic acid

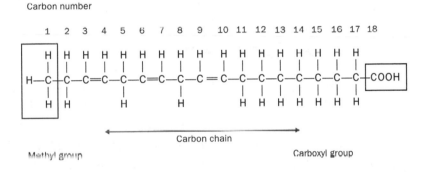

This fatty acid has a *cis-* configuration; both the hydrogens on the double-bonded carbons are on the same side of the molecule. *Cis-* and *trans-* are descriptions of the arrangement of hydrogen atoms around the double bonds. The *cis-* configuration is the one that occurs in nature.

This may seem a trivial point, but the shape of a molecule determines its function. Alter the shape, alter the function. Molecules that are *trans-* versions do not have the same effect in the body as the natural *cis-* version. This has been demonstrated with trans-fatty acids found in margarines and spreads. They may elevate cholesterol just as much as, if not more than, saturated fats.

Essential Fatty Acids

The body can manufacture all of the fatty acids it needs except for the essential fatty acids (EFAs). There are two EFAs: linoleic acid and linolenic acid. (The preceding example was a representation of linolenic acid.) Since the body cannot manufacture EFAs, they must be obtained from the diet.

Conjugated Linoleic Acid

Conjugated linoleic acid (CLA) is an isomer of linoleic acid—which refers to a slight rearrangement of the molecular structure or conjugation. It is found in meat and dairy products, whereas linoleic acid is found in vegetable oils. Since its discovery in 1987, there have been hundreds of articles published on the beneficial effects of this fat.

CLA works as an antioxidant. It can help to reduce inflammation and so may be useful in reducing the cytokine messages that cause the inflammation involved in cachexia. CLA helps to boost the immune system. It can help to decrease insulin resistance so blood glucose levels decrease. It also has been shown to decrease fatty tissue and increase lean muscle tissue.

Our intake of whole milk and red meat is decreasing, and our intake of CLA is decreasing along with it. The only way to get substantial amounts of CLA is to supplement it.

Types of Lipids

How are fatty acids related to the everyday fats and oils we are familiar with? In general, they combine to form lipids (fats) in food.

Triglycerides

Most of the lipids in foods are triglycerides, combinations of four molecules: the glycerol molecule, which acts as a three-"rod" hanger, and the three fatty acids that hang from each "rod" (Figure 6.7). The properties and abilities of each triglyceride depend upon the characteristics of its component fatty acids.

Figure 6.7 Formation of a triglyceride

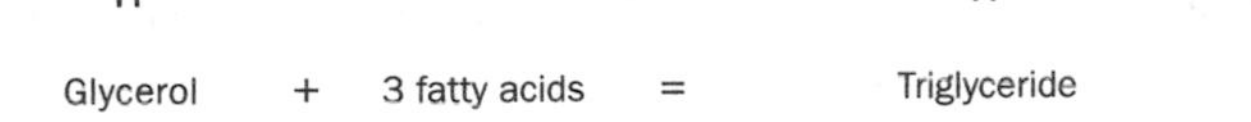

| Glycerol | + | 3 fatty acids | = | Triglyceride |

For example, the properties of an oil are related to the types of triglycerides found in that oil. In turn, the properties of the triglycerides are determined by the fatty acids that form them, and the properties of the fatty acids are determined by their structure. The longer and more unsaturated the fatty acids, the more liquid or soft the fat is at room temperature. The order of the fatty acids on the glycerol molecule also affects the digestibility and absorb-ability of the triglyceride. Because so many different fatty acids are present in natural foods, many types of triglyc-erides are found in a fat or an oil.

When triglycerides are digested by the fat-digesting enzymes (lipases) in the intestine, the fatty acids on the ends are removed, producing a monoglyceride with one fatty acid in the middle, or all of the fatty acids are removed, producing one glycerol hanger and three fatty acids. After absorption the triglycerides are reassembled and pass into the lymphatic system.

Besides triglycerides, foods also contain monoglycerides (with one fatty acid hanging on the glycerol) and diglyc-erides (with two fatty acid molecules). These molecules are also produced during the digestion of triglycerides.

Diglycerides. Diglycerides (DAGs) are fats made up of two fatty acids hanging on a glycerol molecule. A unique type of DAG is the 1,3-diglyceride in which the fatty acid is positioned on either end of the glycerol with the mid-dle position left empty. When this type of fat is digested, it produces one fatty acid and one monoglyceride with the fatty acid located on one end. Normal triglyceride diges-tion produces monoglycerides with the fatty acid located in the middle which intestinal cells are able to reassemble into triglycerides that enter the lymphatic system and bypass the liver. But when that fatty acid is on one end, the cells cannot easily rebuild them into triglycerides. Instead they are broken down into one glycerol molecule and one fatty acid which are then absorbed into the blood and burned for energy in the liver.

This type of DAG is only found in a brand of oil called Enova. Its nutritional profile is similar to that of regular vegetable oil, containing 120 calories and 14 grams of fat per tablespoon. Enova is unsaturated with 8 grams of polyunsaturated fatty acids and 5 grams of monounsaturated fatty acids. Research has shown that Enova oil can help with weight loss. Since it tastes just like vegetable oil, you might want to include it as part of a weight loss diet.

Sterols

Another familiar group of lipids is the sterols; **cholesterol**, the most infamous, is found only in animal foods and is manufactured in the liver. Not all bad, it is the precursor for steroids, including bile acids and the sex hormones. In the liver it can be converted to the precursor of vitamin D, it waterproofs the skin, and it is necessary for proper brain development in infants. However, most of us get too much of a good thing. **β-sitosterol**, found in rice bran, competes with cholesterol for absorption, so it reduces blood cholesterol levels.

Compound Lipids

The final group of lipids consists of the following members:

- **Phospholipids** are compounds of fatty acids, phosphoric acid, and a nitrogen-containing base. One of the most common phospholipids is lecithin.
- **Glycolipids** are compounds of fatty acids, carbohydrate, and a nitrogen-containing base. Glycolipids are part of nerve tissue and certain cell membranes.
- **Sulpholipids** are lipids that contain sulfur.

- **Lipoproteins** are lipids combined with protein. Well-known lipoproteins include chylomicrons, the form in which lipids are packaged to travel in the lymph system to the bloodstream; very low density lipoproteins (VLDLs), the transport packages for triglycerides in the blood; low-density lipoproteins (LDLs), the package that carries cholesterol to the tissues and is commonly referred to as "bad" cholesterol; and high-density lipoproteins (HDLs), the "good" cholesterol that removes cholesterol from the tissues and brings it back to the liver.

Storage of Lipids

Humans have two types of body fat: brown fat and white fat. Most fat is white. It is made of adipose cells that accumulate beneath the skin, around internal organs, and inside muscle tissue. These fat cells store fat as liquid triglycerides.

Brown adipose tissue occurs in much smaller amounts. It decreases with age and is involved in thermogenesis, the response to cold. Brown fat produces energy in the form of heat, warming the body.

Function of Lipids

Although we have a tendency to consider lipids bad, they are necessary for life. Their functions include the following:

- Fats are the most concentrated form of energy. They provide 9 calories for every gram burned, which is more than twice the amount of energy per gram of carbohydrate.
- Adipose (fat) tissue holds organs in place, and the subcutaneous (under the skin) layer of fat provides insulation from the cold and maintains body temperature.
- Fat spares the B vitamin thiamine. Thiamine is required when using carbohydrates for energy.
- Fat spares protein. When fat is present, the body does not have to burn protein for fuel.
- Fat helps in the absorption and transportation of the fat-soluble vitamins A, D, E, and K.
- Lipids slow the rate at which foods leave the stomach. This means that any carbohydrates that are present are not released all at once, keeping insulin and blood sugar levels even.
- Fat decreases the appetite, giving a feeling of satiety.
- Lipids provide the building blocks from which sterols, prostaglandins, thromboxanes, prostacyclins, and cell membranes are made.

Metabolism of Lipids

Fat molecules are too large to be absorbed directly and must be broken down into smaller units. The enzymes responsible for lipid digestion are called **lipases** (*lipo* = fat, *ase* = enzyme). Gastric lipase (*gastric* means "related to the stomach") partially emulsifies and digests the short- and medium-chain fatty acids, and many are absorbed before they have a chance to reach the small intestine.

When fats are detected in the duodenum, bile made in the liver is secreted into the small intestine. Bile is an emulsifying agent. It breaks down fat into small lipid droplets in the same way shampoo emulsifies the oils in your hair. In this way lipids, mainly long-chain fatty acids, are more accessible to the lipases secreted by the pancreas. They are digested to produce monoglycerides, diglycerides, and free fatty acids, which are absorbed into the intestinal wall and then reassembled on the other side into triglycerides.

These triglycerides are packaged into lipoprotein droplets called chylomicrons for transport by the lymphatic system, bypassing the portal vein that takes the water-soluble compounds to the liver. Lymph vessels bring them to the left shoulder, where they are discharged into the bloodstream. Chylomicrons are large enough to make plasma look "milky" after a fat-rich meal.

Lipids include dietary fats and oils. The health properties of an oil are determined by the number of double bonds, the location of the first double bond, and the chain length. Fatty acids with only one double bond are health promoting, while fatty acids without double bonds are not. The two essential fatty acids, linolenic and linoleic acid, can be manipulated to increase or decrease prostaglandin synthesis. Diets that contain more linolenic acid than linoleic acid help the immune system in its fight against cancer.

7

Protein and Cancer

Proteins provide the amino acid building blocks your body needs to build new tissue and repair damaged tissue. In order to quickly repair damage done by cancer treatment, good sources of protein must be eaten each day. The concept of what a good protein is has changed since the 1980s. This chapter will help to update your knowledge as to which sources of protein should be eaten and which should be avoided.

While fats and carbohydrates often suffer from bad press, protein has no such problem. In the public mind, protein is still the most important macronutrient. It is synonymous with strength, victory, and very large muscles. Its name reflects this privileged status. The word *protein* comes from the Greek word meaning "of first importance." In reality, protein must share the spotlight with fats and carbohydrates. No one macronutrient is more important than any other.

Like carbohydrates and lipids, protein is made up of carbon, oxygen, and hydrogen atoms. Protein differs in that it also contains a nitrogen atom. Protein is the major structural molecule of the body. Twenty to thirty pounds of an adult's total weight is protein, with half of that being found in the muscles.

All enzymes are proteins. Many hormones are proteins. The only constituents of the body that do not contain protein are urine and bile. Proteins are made up of chains of **amino acids** (*amine* = nitrogen-containing).

Protein Molecule Shape

Twenty-two different amino acids are present in the human body. Each amino acid is joined to the other by means of a peptide bond forming peptide or polypeptide chains. Chemically each amino acid is composed of an amino group, a carboxyl group (*oxyl* = contains oxygen), a hydrogen atom, and the remainder of the molecule, R, which differentiates it from other types (Figure 7.1). The R group can range in size from twenty-three to several hundred thousand amino groups. The twenty-two amino acids identified in the body form a sort of alphabet. Each amino acid "letter" can be used to make up an unlimited number of protein words.

Figure 7.1 Amino acid

COOH — Carboxyl group

H—C—R² — Remaining section of molecule

NH₂ — Amino group

What your body does with the protein is determined by the shape of the protein. Chains of polypeptides are twisted together to form a coil that resembles a Slinky toy. The hydrogen atoms in the Slinky form an effective but weak bond between turns of the coil. As long as the hydrogen bonds are intact, the protein holds its coil shape. These coils are then arranged into a specific shape that determines what the body uses it for.

Simple but long arrangements are called fibrous proteins. These proteins are used to make structural parts of tissue, including the collagen in connective tissue, the keratin in hair and nails, and the myosin in muscles. Fibrous proteins do not dissolve in water and are very strong structurally.

If the chain is twisted after it forms a Slinky, it folds into itself, forming a kind of knot. In a peptide coil this knot is held in place by the sulfur-to-sulfur bonds found in some of the amino acids. Slinky knots are called globular proteins. Globular proteins form enzymes and are present in the extracellular fluid of plants and animals. They dissolve easily in water. This is the kind of protein found in egg whites, the casein of milk, the hemoglobin of red blood cells, and the albumins and globulins of blood plasma.

When a protein enters the digestive tract, it cannot be absorbed until it has been broken down into its amino acid components. This is done by **hydrolysis** (Figure 7.2), or the breakage of peptide bonds by the addition of a molecule of water. This produces smaller proteins: individual amino acids, dipeptides (two amino acid proteins), and tripeptides (three amino acid proteins), which are easily

Figure 7.2 (a) Formation of a peptide bond
(b) hydrolysis, or breakage of a peptide bond

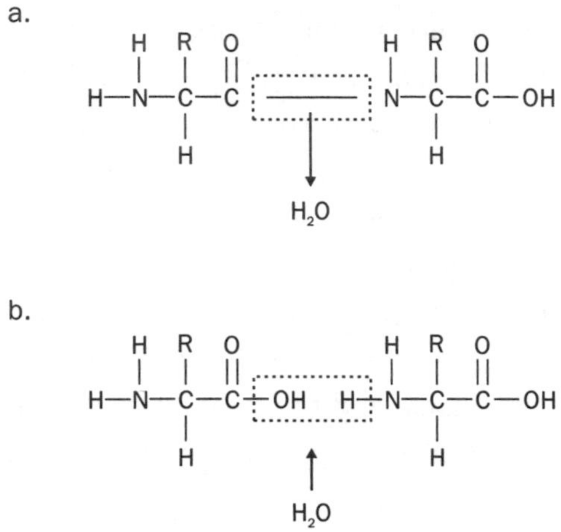

a.

H_2O

b.

H_2O

absorbed by the digestive tract. (Conversely, a peptide bond is formed by removing a molecule of water from two adjacent amino acids.)

The peptide bond can easily be attacked by the digestive enzymes of bacteria. The bacterial growth and formation of potentially toxic proteins as by-products are the cause of food spoilage. This is why protein foods such as milk, eggs, meat, poultry, and fish must be refrigerated.

Essential and Nonessential Amino Acids

The body can manufacture most of the amino acids it needs from carbohydrates, fat, and other amino acids.

Types of Amino Acids

Nonessential Amino Acids

Alanine	Hydroxyglutamic acid
Arginine	Hydroxyproline
Aspartic acid	Norleucine
Citrulline	Proline
Glycine	Serine
Glutamic acid	Cystine

Essential Amino Acids

Histidine	Phenylalanine
Isoleucine	Threonine
Leucine	Tryptophan
Lysine	Tyrosine
Methionine	Valine

These are called nonessential amino acids. This is a somewhat inaccurate term, since the nonessential amino acids are essential for life. They are nonessential only in the sense that they do not have to be obtained from the diet.

Ten other amino acids cannot be manufactured in amounts needed to support growth and maintenance. These are the essential amino acids, and they must be obtained from the diet. Without them, protein cannot be made and body tissues cannot be maintained. When you are sick or recovering from surgery, your need for the essential amino acids increases.

Leucine, isoleucine, and valine are sometimes called the branched-chain amino acids (BCAAs). The phrase "branched–chain" refers to their molecular structure. This type of amino acid is found in large amounts in muscle tissue. Supplementing the BCAAs may increase appetite and thus be useful in treating cachexia.

Functions of Amino Acids

Besides forming the building blocks of protein, each amino acid has other specific functions in the body. Tryptophan is a precursor of (used to make) niacin, a B vitamin, and serotonin, a neurotransmitter in the brain. Methionine provides sulfur groups for protein manufacture and detoxification of toxins by the liver. Phenylalanine is a precursor of the amino acid tyrosine, used to make hair and skin pigment. Histidine is used to make histamine, a chemical that dilates blood vessels, and glycine, which combines with toxic chemicals and makes them harmless. Glutamic acid is a precursor of gamma-aminobutyric acid (GABA), a neurotransmitter.

Complete and Incomplete Proteins

The concept of "complete" and "incomplete" protein is one of the most confusing notions in nutrition. It was developed in an age when animal protein was considered the gold standard of protein quality. Today the ideas of complete and incomplete protein have taken on an entirely new meaning.

The so-called complete proteins contain all ten of the essential amino acids in sufficient quantities to allow growth in a young animal. Not surprisingly, ovalbumin, the main protein in eggs, and casein, the main protein in milk, are complete proteins. The protein found in animal flesh is also complete. In the unlikely event that you are dependent on only a single food for survival, it would have to be a complete protein source. This situation, however, rarely occurs except in infancy.

The amino acids obtained from the diet are combined in the body with amino acids recycled from internal tissue breakdown. It is from this amino acid pool that the tissues draw their protein for new cells. The notion of protein combining—the belief that complementary proteins must be eaten at the same meal or a protein deficiency will ensue—has been thoroughly disproven.

Complete proteins also come packaged with "complete fats." Since saturated fat is an absolute necessity for infant brain development and growth, complete-protein foods are likely to be excellent sources of unneeded artery-clogging saturated fats.

Incomplete proteins, on the other hand, lack these saturated fats. Like the complete proteins, they contain all eleven of the essential amino acids. The only difference is that the amounts of these amino acids differ from food to food, in much the same way vitamin and mineral levels vary.

Incomplete protein sources are superior to complete protein sources. Plant proteins are usually low in total fat and saturated fat; they are free of cholesterol. The high-fat sources of incomplete protein, such as nuts and seeds, contain heart-healthy fats that combat tumor spread, reduce inflammation, and prevent weight loss. They are also excellent sources of cancer-fighting fiber, minerals, vitamins, and phytochemicals.

Nitrogen Balance

True protein deficiencies are very rare and do not occur in the healthy, well-nourished individual. Protein-calorie malnutrition is a condition caused by not getting enough food to maintain health. This can result from much higher than normal protein needs or from an inability to absorb the protein that is eaten.

Nitrogen balance is a term you are likely to hear used by your physician or nutritionist. Since protein is the only nitrogen-containing macronutrient, the amount of nitrogen in the body is an accurate method of determining protein content of the body. When the amount of protein present in the diet is known and the amount of protein being excreted is known, then the amount of protein left in the body can be measured.

When nitrogen intake and nitrogen output are equal, an individual is said to be in nitrogen balance, or equilibrium. This is the usual state for healthy adults.

If an individual has more nitrogen coming in than going out, that person is said to be in positive nitrogen balance. This means the buildup of tissue is greater than the breakdown of tissue. This occurs in pregnant and lactating women; growing infants, children, and adolescents; and adults who are recovering from an illness that resulted in a protein loss.

A negative nitrogen balance indicates that the opposite is happening; more nitrogen is leaving than is coming in. The rate of tissue breakdown is greater than the rate of tissue synthesis. This occurs when the body is not taking in enough protein, protein is being burned for energy because not enough fat and carbohydrates are present for fuel, or the protein needs of the body are greatly increased, as in cancer.

Cancer and Protein

Cancer cells change the metabolism of protein so that more amino acids are available for tumor growth. This can translate into a loss of muscle tissue and predisposes cancer patients to a state of negative nitrogen balance. You can also lose muscle tissue just through bed rest.

Most of the protein in your diet should come from plant sources. Plant proteins come complete with numerous cancer-fighting nutrients and phytochemicals. The proteins from fatty fish come packaged with the omega-3 fatty acids necessary for the body's defense system. They should provide the second highest amount of protein in your diet. Skinless poultry should make the smallest contribution to your amino acid pool. Poultry is a good source of minerals but often tastes "wrong" from the effects of chemotherapy and radiation. An alternative to fish is organic, grass-fed beef, which is also high in the omega-3 fatty acids.

Proteins are composed of amino acids and are the body's only source of nitrogen. They contribute to the formation of body tissues, enzymes, antibodies, hemoglobin, and hormones. Cancer interferes with protein metabolism by burning some of the body's proteins for fuel even when enough carbohydrates and fat are present. A lack of protein has a devastating effect on the immune system.

8

Vitamins and Cancer

Vitamins, minerals, and trace minerals are called **micronutrients** because the body requires them in only small amounts, unlike the **macronutrients** (carbohydrates, proteins, fat, and water). They are essential components in enzymes and coenzymes, and many serve as antioxidants. This chapter describes the role of the fat- and water-soluble vitamins and explores their relationship to cancer growth and ways they can aid in cancer treatment.

When nutrition was a young science, researchers found that a synthetic diet of carbohydrates, lipids, proteins, water, and minerals was not enough to allow animals to grow and thrive. This led to the discovery of a group of unrelated carbon-containing compounds called vitamins. **Vitamins** are defined as organic substances, needed in small amounts, that perform at least one specific metabolic function and must be obtained from the diet.

The word *vitamin* was coined in 1912 by Casimir Funk. Originally vitamins were recognized only for their ability to prevent deficiency diseases. For example, vitamin C was discovered because of its ability to cure scurvy. With time this definition has proved too narrow. Vitamins are now known to serve many functions in the body besides preventing specific deficiency diseases. For example, many vitamins are also potent antioxidants, and some vitamins enhance the absorption of other vitamins or minerals.

Your cell citizens obtain vitamins in three ways:

- They can absorb vitamins from foods in the digestive tract.
- Some bacteria in the colon produce vitamins (such as vitamin K), and these can also be absorbed.
- The body is able to manufacture some vitamins, such as vitamin D.

Vitamins do not provide energy or contribute to cell mass. They prefer to be "the molecules behind the nutrients," so to speak—helper elements that enable other nutrients from the sidelines. Each individual vitamin is actually a family of related compounds, including precursors and bound forms. Some substances, such as choline, carnitine, inostitol, taurine, and pyrroloquinoline quinone, have vitamin-like properties and may be required at particular stages of growth.

Dietary Reference Intake

In the United States, the Food and Nutrition Board of the Institutes of Medicine establishes dietary standards. This board has replaced the old recommended dietary allowance (RDA) with the new **dietary reference intake (DRI)**.

The levels of some nutrients in the DRI are higher than in the RDA. This represents a shift from recommendations based on preventing deficiency diseases to recommendations based on preventing chronic diseases. The reference dose is defined as "an estimate (with uncertainty spanning perhaps an order of magnitude) of a daily exposure to the human population, including sensitive subgroups, that is likely to be without an appreciable risk of deleterious effects over a lifetime." When considering the DRI, keep these factors in mind:

- The *D* in DRI stands for "dietary" not "daily." You do not need to eat the DRI for each nutrient each day.
- The *R* stands for "reference" not "recommended." The values are meant as guidelines not requirements.
- The DRIs are guidelines for populations not individuals.
- The DRIs are also guidelines for healthy populations and not those with a chronic disease such as cancer who may need additional nutrients.

For example, the DRI for niacin is 16 milligrams, but that does not mean your body needs 16 milligrams of niacin every day; even the water-soluble vitamins have short-term stores. It does not mean that the government is recommending that you, a person with high cholesterol, get 16 milligrams of niacin. It does means that a healthy *population* should be getting 16 milligrams of niacin. The DRIs, just like the RDAs, were designed to be used by nutrition professionals rather than laypeople, but you can expect to read about them as they become more commonly used. Understand what they are so you will recognize when they are abused.

The Water-Soluble Vitamins

Vitamins that can dissolve in water are called water soluble. They include the B complex vitamins and vitamin C. Water-soluble vitamins are absorbed into the bloodstream via the portal system and taken immediately to the liver before distribution to the body. The body does not store water-soluble vitamins. To keep optimal levels of these nutrients in blood circulation, you need to eat their food sources frequently. Most of the B vitamins function as parts of enzymes. All can be excreted in the urine.

The B Complex Vitamins

The B complex vitamins are known for two major functions: first, they are an absolute necessity for the conversion of carbohydrates into glucose, the body's main energy source. Second, they are essential for the proper functioning of the nervous system. In addition, the B vitamins help to strengthen cellular membranes, fortifying them against stress.

The B complex vitamins share a close relationship. A deficiency in one may impair the use of the others, and supplementation of one may cause a deficiency in the others. That is why the B complex should be considered one

How to Supplement the B Vitamins

- If a supplement is necessary, take a balanced B complex. If you are allergic or sensitive to yeast, look for a yeast-free supplement.
- Always take a B complex supplement on a full stomach. Otherwise stomach irritation can occur. You will know the supplement is being absorbed when your urine takes on a bright yellow color.
- Do not buy a time-release B complex supplement. Each B vitamin is absorbed in a different area of the gastrointestinal tract. The vitamins released past their absorption point will be lost in the feces.
- If you need to supplement only one particular B vitamin, also take a B complex supplement as a base.
- Very large doses of some B vitamins can cause liver damage. Have your health care provider perform regular liver function tests.

vitamin rather than a group of single nutrients. Never take megadoses of one particular B vitamin without medical supervision. Like the other water-soluble vitamins, the B vitamins are not stored in large amounts. This has been misinterpreted to mean that excess will "wash away" in the urine. Like all substances, the B vitamins must be detoxified before the kidney can excrete them.

Sources of B vitamins include brewer's yeast (nutritional yeast), whole grains and cereals, wheat and rice bran and germ, beans, nuts and seeds, milk, eggs, and leafy green vegetables.

Thiamine, or vitamin B₁. During absorption, thiamine is converted to thiamine pyrophosphate. In this active form, thiamine is involved with energy production and nerve maintenance and conduction. Thiamine is lost when grains are refined. Deficiency can cause a lack of appetite, irritability, fatigue, depression, sleep disorders, and weight loss.

Sources of thiamine include brewer's yeast, almonds, wheat germ, nuts, beans, whole grains, split peas, mung beans, and lentils.

Riboflavin, riboflavin phosphate, or vitamin B₂. Riboflavin is a critical part of flavin mononucleotide and flavin adenine dinucleotide, coenzymes involved in energy production. The production of these enzymes from riboflavin can be affected by hormones and drugs. Thyroid hormones and adrenal steroids enhance their production, and tricyclic antidepressants and phenothiazines inhibit their production. The need for riboflavin increases with energy intake and growth needs. When B complex is taken as a food supplement, the breakdown products of riboflavin give the urine a bright yellow color and pungent odor.

Sources of riboflavin include brewer's yeast, almonds, wheat germ, wild rice, mushrooms, millet, mackerel, soybeans, eggs, and split peas.

Niacin, nicotinamide, or nicotinic acid. Niacin is an essential component of nicotinamide adenine dinucleotide and nicotinamide adenine dinucleotide phosphate, coenzymes needed for metabolism. It is absorbed from the diet and can also be manufactured by the body from the amino acid tryptophan. Niacin is available in a time-release form that does not cause the "flushing" effect seen in regular supplements. However, this time-release form has been linked to liver damage, so it should never be taken in high doses or for prolonged periods.

Sources of niacin include brewer's yeast, wheat bran, peanuts, sunflower and sesame seeds, pine nuts, brown rice, and seed oils.

Pyridoxine, pyridoxal, pyridoxamine, or vitamin B_6. In the tissues, all forms of vitamin B_6 are converted to pyridoxal 5-phosphate, a coenzyme necessary for fat and protein metabolism and also immune functioning. Pyridoxal 5-phosphate is necessary for the proper metabolism of the amino acid tryptophan. It is a necessary part of more than one hundred enzyme systems.

Vitamin B_6 is necessary for the immune system, where it is involved in antibody production. A deficiency of pyridoxine reduces the number of disease-fighting lymphocytes and lowers the ability of other immune elements to respond to the chemical messengers sent by the lymphocytes. Food processing can destroy some of the B_6 present in foods. Pregnancy, lactation, an overactive thyroid, or a high intake of animal protein can cause a need for extra B_6.

Sources of pyridoxine include brewer's yeast, sunflower seeds, wheat germ, tuna, beans, salmon, trout, mackerel, brown rice, bananas, halibut, walnuts, hazelnuts, avocados, egg yolks, and kale.

Folic acid, folacin, folate, or tetrahydrofolic acid. Folic acid is the commonly used term for pteroyl-polyglutamic acid, the precursor of a large family of folate compounds.

It is needed for RNA synthesis. A deficiency of this vitamin causes megoblastic anemia and has been associated with a degeneration of the intestinal lining, which then further reduces nutrient absorption. Folic acid may help block dysplasia, a condition in which cells that have begun to divide rapidly may become malignant. Even a mild folic acid deficiency may promote cervical dysplasia.

The body cannot make any folate and therefore must obtain all it needs from the diet. Folates are very sensitive to heat. Boiling, steaming, or frying for five to ten minutes may destroy up to 96 percent of the folate in a food.

Sources of folic acid include brewer's yeast, black-eyed peas, wheat and rice germ and bran, beans, soy foods, lentils, asparagus, leafy green vegetables, green cruciferous vegetables, whole wheat, oatmeal, barley, almonds, walnuts, and split peas.

Vitamin B₁₂, or cobalamin. In the stomach, cobalamin is released from its dietary sources by peptic digestion. Cells in the stomach lining produce a substance called intrinsic factor (IF), which binds to the vitamin, forming an IF-cobalamin complex. This complex is resistant to digestion and is readily absorbed in the small intestine.

Vitamin B_{12} is involved in protein, fat, and carbohydrate metabolism. Older people do not always produce enough intrinsic factor, making absorption difficult. Microorganisms are the ultimate source of all vitamin B_{12} in the diet. Strict vegans may have to supplement this nutrient.

Sources of vitamin B_{12} include shellfish, fish, egg yolks, skinless poultry, yogurt, and milk.

Biotin. Biotin is essential for many enzyme systems. It is present in most foods and can be made by intestinal bacteria and absorbed from there. It is resistant to heat and related metabolically to B_{12}, folate, and pantothenic acid.

Sources of biotin include mushrooms, egg yolks, bananas, grapefruit, watermelon, and strawberries.

Pantothenic acid. A part of coenzyme A, pantothenic acid is involved in the release of energy from carbohydrates and in the breakdown and use of fatty acids. It also reduces stress. Milling cereal grains reduces their pantothenic acid content by 50 percent.

Sources of pantothenic acid include eggs, salmon, whole-grain cereals, legumes, brewer's yeast, cauliflower, broccoli, potatoes, tomatoes, and molasses.

Vitamin C, Ascorbic Acid

Perhaps the most famous and favorite vitamin is vitamin C. It is the antioxidant responsible for protecting the watery parts of the cell from free radical damage. Vitamin C prevents the oxidation of folate, thereby increasing the amount of folate available to the body. It enhances the absorption of iron and the bioavailablity of stored iron. For example, when a vitamin C source such as orange juice is ingested with a slice of whole-wheat bread, the iron in the bread becomes free for absorption. Humans are among the few mammals unable to make their own vitamin C. Most other mammals are able to manufacture their own supplies as needed.

Vitamin C detoxifies histamine, which can suppress the immune system. It helps build dense connective tissue, which may inhibit tumor invasion, and research shows that it enhances antibiotic therapy. The emotional and

> ## How to Supplement Vitamin C
>
> Ascorbic acid is easily lost in the urine, so avoid taking the recommended dose all at once. This will cause the blood levels of vitamin C to rise and then plummet. Take vitamin C in smaller doses throughout the day, or buy a time-release capsule or sustained-release tablet.
>
> For best absorption, take vitamin C with food. Consider taking a form of vitamin C that includes the bioflavonoids, which work with it synergistically.

physical stress of having cancer may increase your body's use of vitamin C.

Sources of vitamin C include sweet peppers, kale, collard and turnip greens, broccoli, strawberries, papaya, citrus fruits, mangoes, cantaloupe, and cabbage.

Fat-Soluble Nutrients

Fat-soluble vitamins are intimately related to lipids. They need fat to be absorbed, and when cancer treatment interferes with fat absorption, a deficiency of these vitamins may occur.

There are four families of fat-soluble vitamins: vitamin A, vitamin D, vitamin E, and vitamin K. These vitamins need to be dissolved in fat before they can be absorbed in the intestine. Low-fat and low-calorie diets, whether by chance or on purpose, risk not providing enough of these vitamins.

Dietary fats and the fat-soluble vitamins are absorbed into the lymph vessels, bypassing the portal blood system that takes water-soluble nutrients to the liver. After a long climb up to your shoulder, they are dumped into the left subclavian artery.

Vitamins A and D can be toxic in large amounts when taken over a long period. They are stored in fatty tissues and the liver, and they can accumulate over time. Unlike vitamin C and the B complex, the fat-soluble vitamins are very stable. They are better able to stand up to the heat of cooking and processing.

Vitamin A, Retinol, Retinal, Retinoic Acid, Retinyl Esters

The vitamin A (or retinol) family contains several forms, both natural and synthetic, that have vitamin A activity. Some of these are compounds found in vegetable foods that the body can convert into vitamin A, such as the alpha-, beta-, and gamma-carotenes. Absorption of retinol requires bile, pancreatic enzymes, and antioxidants; in the form of retinoic acid, it is absorbed directly. A six-month supply of vitamin A is stored in the liver as retinyl esters. Vitamin A levels are decreased in patients who are receiving chemotherapy.

Retinol is necessary for eye function. It protects your mucus membranes and reduces the risk of infection. With regard to cancer, vitamin A can promote differentiation in epithelial cells and remission of premalignant oral lesions (leukoplakias). It also inhibits the development of cancerous tumors. A lack of vitamin A will decrease antibody formation, while vitamin A supplementation increases the cytotoxic action of T cells, NK cells, and macrophages.

Retinol can be toxic in dosages of more than 15,000 RE, but much of this toxicity can be prevented by also taking vitamin E. Vitamins E and A work together.

You may be confused by the different means of expressing retinol levels.

In the past, the RDA for retinol was expressed in International Units (IU), which has now been replaced by retinol equivalents (RE). Not all labels reflect this change.

- Micrograms (mcg) measure the weight of retinol; 1 mcg of retinol = 1 RE
- 3.33 IU of retinol = 1 RE
- Beta carotene is preformed retinol; 10 IU of beta-carotene = 1 RE

This means that when a label claims to contain 20,000 IU of beta carotene, it translates into 2,000 RE. A supplement that contains 20 mcg of retinol translates into 20 RE.

Vitamin D, Cholecalciferol (D₃), Ergosterol (D₂), Calcitriol

The vitamin D family has two possible sources: preformed from the diet and synthesized by the skin. Vitamin D is called the sunshine vitamin, because the large amounts of the precursor 7-dehydrocholesterol in the skin, when exposed to the ultraviolet light from the sun, are con-

---

Tips for Using Supplements

When purchasing fat-soluble vitamins and supplements, be sure they are fresh. If the supplements are past or close to the pull date on the bottles, do not purchase them. Oils must be very fresh to neutralize free radicals. Rancid oils—ones that smell fishy or like Play Doh—are old and inactive and can cause more free radicals in the body. Store oils and fat-soluble supplements in the refrigerator, inside airtight containers. Keep them out of direct sunlight as much as possible.

---

verted into cholecalciferol (vitamin D_3). It is estimated that up to 80 percent of the body's needs for vitamin D can be obtained this way. How much is produced depends on how much melanin pigment is in the skin (melanin competes with the precursor for the light), how much skin is exposed, and how much sun reaches the skin. This means that dark-skinned people who live in cold climates (reducing the skin area exposed to the sun) and anyone who lives in low-sun areas (Seattle or England, for example) probably cannot rely on manufacturing enough of their own vitamin D. The elderly are also at risk, since they often cannot get out and do not eat fortified foods.

Vitamin D is a hormone that regulates mineral balance. It stimulates intestinal absorption of calcium and phosphorus, works with the parathyroid hormone to mobilize calcium from bone, and stimulates the reabsorption of calcium from the kidneys. It also plays a role in cellular differentiation and development.

Sources of vitamin D include sunshine, fortified cows' milk and soy milk, deep-sea fish and fish oils, and egosterol in plants.

Vitamin E, Tocopherol, Tocotrienol

The vitamin E family is a group of eight closely related fat-soluble compounds made up of four tocopherols (alpha, beta, delta, gamma) and four tocotrienols. Vitamin E is stored in all areas of the body in fatty deposits, the liver, and muscle. Eating a lot of linoleic acid and polyunsaturated fatty acids decreases the amount of vitamin E absorbed by reducing the micelle formation that is necessary for absorption. Vitamin E is an antioxidant. It works in partnership with vitamin C, protecting the lipids in the cell as vitamin C protects the watery contents. It protects vitamins A, C, and the carotenes from oxidation.

Vitamin E may protect healthy cells from some of the toxicity of radiation therapy and decrease the toxicity of certain chemotherapy drugs. It also appears to stimulate the immune system and protect the lipids in the cell membrane from damage.

Sources of vitamin E include wheat germ oil, germ from cereals, egg yolks, and nuts.

Vitamin K, Phylloquinone (K_1), Menaquinone (K_2), Menadione (Synthetic Form of K_3)

Vitamin K_1 is found in green plants, while vitamin K_2 is produced by bacteria in the colon. In the liver vitamin K acts as a coenzyme in reactions that produce the clotting factors and can interfere with the anticlotting effects of anticoagulants. However, at doses lower than 1 milligram per day, vitamin K_1 does not pose a threat and may actually enhance the antimetastatic effects of anticoagulants. Vitamin K may also act as a toxin to cancer cells while not harming normal cells.

Sources of vitamin K include cabbage, broccoli, turnip greens, lettuce, wheat bran, cheese, and egg yolks.

Vitamins are organic compounds that serve as helpers to other nutrients in the biochemical processes of digestion, absorption, and metabolism. There are two types: water soluble and fat soluble. The water-soluble vitamins are particularly vulnerable to light, heat, and air. Therefore, fresh, raw fruits and vegetables have higher concentrations of the water-soluble vitamins than cooked or aged produce.

The four fat-soluble vitamin families—A, D, E, and K—are often depleted in cancer patients. This is usually caused by fat malabsorption. These vitamins are often difficult to obtain in the diet, and a low-dose supplement can be very helpful in rebuilding stores. Vitamin E is a nontoxic antioxidant that protects the other fat-soluble vitamins and oils from oxidation. It can be taken in larger doses and should always accompany any supplemented oils (such as flaxseed or fish oil) and the other fat-soluble vitamins.

9

Minerals and Cancer

Minerals are the elements in simple inorganic form. Mineral elements that the body needs in large amounts are called the macrominerals. Those needed in small amounts are called the trace minerals, and those needed in minute amounts are the ultratrace minerals. More than twenty-two minerals are considered to be essential, with more identified as science progresses. This chapter describes the role of minerals in the diet, especially for people with cancer.

Minerals may take the form of ions (atoms that carry an electrical charge) or salts. Metals form positive ions (cations), and nonmetals form negative ions (anions). Metal cations include sodium, potassium, magnesium, and calcium. Nonmetal anions include chlorine (chloride), sulfur (sulfate), phosphorus (phosphate), and bicarbonate. A salt is formed from a metal and a nonmetal. The most familiar salt is sodium chloride, or common table salt.

In bones and teeth, minerals are found in the form of salts (mainly as calcium and phosphates). In solution, salts dissolve. They are found in the bodily fluids as Na^+

(sodium), K^+ (potassium), Ca^{++} (calcium), Cl^- (chloride), and $H_2PO_4^{-2}$ (phosphate).

$$NaCl + H_2O \rightarrow Na^+ + Cl^-$$
Salt dissolves in water

In cancer patients mineral deficiencies can result from several factors:

- Decreased mineral intake from loss of appetite or the poor selection of foods
- Decreased absorption as the result of radiation-damaged villi, bowel inflammation, or not enough pancreatic enzymes
- Decreased utilization of minerals due to drug interactions or too little energy from food
- Increased losses of minerals due to diarrhea, vomiting, or drug therapy
- Increased requirement due to tumor growth

The Macrominerals

There are seven macrominerals: calcium, phosphorus, magnesium, sulfur, sodium, potassium, and chloride.

Calcium and Phosphorus

Calcium and phosphorus are closely related, so we will discuss them together. Calcium is the most abundant mineral in the body, comprising 39 percent of the minerals present. Of this calcium, 99 percent is stored in the bones, teeth, and hard tissues. The remaining 1 percent is found in the tissues and extracellular fluid, where it is very active metabolically.

Phosphorus is the second most abundant mineral. Eighty percent of it is found in the bones and teeth. The remaining 20 percent is distributed to every cell of the body and extracellular fluid, where it is involved in numerous chemical reactions.

In bone, calcium and phosphorus are present as calcium carbonate and calcium phosphate. These two salts are arranged together in a crystal structure around a matrix of softer protein material. This structure is called hydroxyapatite. It provides strength and hardness to the bone.

Calcium is also needed for certain enzymes involved in energy production, for proper blood clotting, and muscle contraction. It affects transportation across cellular and subcellular membranes. It influences the release of neurotransmitters and the release and activation of enzymes. Calcium is required for nerve transmission and to regulate the heartbeat.

Phosphorus is the most active of the minerals. It is involved in almost every metabolic function of the body. In its most important function, phosphate acts as an energy currency. This energy is stored in a rechargeable battery known as adenosine triphosphate (ATP). When energy is needed for a chemical reaction, an ATP molecule comes to the site from the mitochondria. The needed energy is stored in one of the phosphate-to-carbon bonds. The ATP molecule breaks the bond, and the energy is freed for the chemical reaction. What is left is adenosine diphosphate (ADP) and a free phosphate group. ADP molecules and free phosphate groups wander back to the mitochondria, where they are recharged with the energy released from burning glucose.

Several factors increase the body's absorption of calcium and phosphate:

- *Acidity of the gastric juice.* The hydrochloric acid present in the stomach lowers the pH (increases the acidity) of the chyme (undigested food) in the digestive tract to a level that is more favorable to calcium and phosphate absorption.
- *Fat intake.* When fat is present in the digestive tract, it slows the movement of chyme, giving more time for mineral absorption.
- *Protein intake.* A high intake of protein favors a higher absorption of calcium and phosphorus.
- *Vitamin D.* The active form of vitamin D stimulates intestinal absorption.
- *State of need.* When calcium levels are low, the body will absorb it more efficiently. When more calcium is needed for growth, it is better absorbed. As the body ages, the absorption decreases.

Phosphorus is so widely distributed in the food supply that it is almost impossible not to get enough. A much bigger problem is the large amounts of phosphorus taken in as phosphates in prepared foods and sodas. Too many phosphates causes an imbalance, leading to a loss of calcium through the urine. The phosphorus in unrefined foods poses no threat.

Sources of calcium include fortified soy milk, fortified orange juice, nonfat dairy products, tofu, corn tortillas, collard and turnip greens, kale, and broccoli.

Magnesium

Magnesium is the atom responsible for the green color of chlorophyll. Therefore, if a vegetable is green, it is a source of magnesium.

Magnesium and calcium have similar functions and may oppose each other. In normal muscle contraction, calcium stimulates and magnesium relaxes. The presence of calcium, fat, alcohol, phosphates, and phytates decreases magnesium absorption. As dietary calcium is decreased, magnesium absorption is increased. The kidneys regulate magnesium excretion. When the level of magnesium intake is low, the kidneys reabsorb most of the magnesium so that very little is lost.

A deficiency in magnesium can be caused by not enough intake, persistent vomiting (the gastric juice is relatively high in magnesium which is normally totally reabsorbed), or rapid transport of food through the digestive tract. Both alcohol and diuretics increase the loss of magnesium through the urine.

Sources of magnesium include nuts, brewer's yeast, soybeans, dried apricots, collard greens, and whole-grain cereals.

Sulfur

Sulfur is present in every cell of the body. The highest concentrations are in the hair, skin, and nails. It has several functions:

- Sulfur is a part of three vitamins: thiamine, pantothenic acid, and biotin.

- Sulfur compounds act as detoxifying agents by combining with toxic substances and converting them into harmless ones which are then excreted.
- Sulfur is involved in the formation of blood clots and in the transfer of energy.

Sulfur is obtained primarily through the amino acids methionine and cysteine. Any excess of organic sulfur is excreted in the urine.

Electrolytes

Sodium, potassium, and chloride are known collectively as the electrolytes. Electrolytes carry the electrical currents for all the cells of the body. There must be a perfect balance of electrolytes for proper muscle movement, brain activity, and heart functions. Vomiting and diarrhea can seriously deplete electrolytes and in rare cases cause life-threatening complications.

The Trace Minerals

The trace minerals include iron, zinc, copper, selenium, and chromium. The remaining trace minerals—iodine, manganese, cobalt, arsenic, boron, molybdenum, nickel, silicon, vanadium, cadmium, lead, lithium, bromine, fluorine, and tin—have only begun to be studied. It is known that they are needed in minute amounts, and some, such as lead and cadmium, may even be poisonous if taken in excess. In general the best sources of trace minerals are whole foods and particularly whole grains.

Iron

The red in the red blood cells comes from iron. As the active compound in hemoglobin, it is the carrier of oxygen from the lungs to the tissues and the carrier of carbon dioxide from the tissues back to the lungs. Iron is the reason muscles are red. It is also the active part of myoglobin, the iron-containing compound that provides oxygen to muscle cells. It is an important part of many different enzymes.

The combination of foods eaten influences the amount of iron absorbed. The iron in cereal grains is bound to phytic acid, forming an insoluble iron-phytate complex. When a vitamin C source is ingested along with the grain, this complex is broken, freeing both the iron and the phytic acid (which is linked to decreased cancer risk as well). Iron losses occur from loss of blood due to menstruation or minute bleeding in the intestine. For example, each 500 milligrams of aspirin a person takes can cause the loss of up to 1 teaspoon of blood.

Follow these tips to help increase iron absorption:

- Eat a small amount (1 or 2 tablespoons) of fish or skinless poultry with a meal.
- Cook in an iron pot. It can add substantial amounts of dietary iron, particularly when the food being cooked is acidic, such as tomato sauce.
- Eat foods rich in malic, ascorbic, or citric acid.

Iron-Rich Foods

Food	Iron Content (milligrams)
Clams, canned, 3 ounces	12.8
Sunflower seeds, kernels, ½ cup	4.9
Oyster, cooked, 3 ounces	4.4
Cashews, ½ cup	4.1
Shrimp, boiled, 3½ ounces	3.1
Lentils, cooked, ½ cup	3.1
Potato, baked with skin, 1 medium	2.8
Kidney beans, cooked, ½ cup	2.6
Almonds, ½ cup	2.5
Refried beans, cooked, ½ cup	2.2
Prunes, dried, 10	2.1
Trout, baked or broiled, 3 ounces	2.1
Turkey, roasted, dark meat, 3 ounces	2.0
Black beans, cooked, ½ cup	1.8
Apricot halves, dried, ½ cup	1.7
Artichoke, 1 whole	1.6
Peas, cooked, ½ cup	1.6
Raisins, ½ cup	1.5
Chicken, roasted, dark meat, 3 ounces	1.1

- Avoid coffee, tea, and spinach with iron-rich meals. These foods contain compounds that decrease mineral absorption.

Zinc

The trace mineral zinc is vital for the metabolism of vitamin A and has important roles in many of the body's systems, including immune function and wound healing. Dietary zinc is necessary for the working of many metal-containing enzymes, the stabilization of membranes, and growth.

In people with cancer, low levels of zinc can reduce the ability to taste. This can contribute to a lack of appetite during treatment. Low zinc levels can slow wound healing from surgery and tissue regrowth of radiation- and chemotherapy-damaged tissues. Insufficient zinc affects T cell and NK cell activity, thereby decreasing the ability of the immune system to defend itself. Zinc is necessary for the proper use of insulin, the hormone that regulates blood sugar. This is important for people with cancer, because the disease alters blood sugar metabolism.

Whole grains are much better sources of zinc (and other minerals) than refined. Even though the zinc from refined grains is better absorbed than the zinc from whole grains, the whole grain contains more zinc to begin with. Zinc supplements should be taken between meals separately from other supplements to prevent them from competing for absorption.

Sources of zinc include nuts, whole grains, shellfish, split peas, lima beans, sardines, anchovies, haddock, turnips, potatoes, egg yolks, soy lecithin, almonds, walnuts, and garlic.

Copper

Copper plays an important but poorly understood role in iron metabolism. In fact, anemia was first described as a copper deficiency. Copper is necessary for the proper functioning of the immune system, and animal studies have linked copper deficiency with decreased activity of NK cells. It is a part of superoxide dismutase, an enzyme necessary for protection from free radicals.

How well copper is absorbed depends on what a meal contains. The high doses of vitamin C we recommend will decrease the absorption of copper, so you must take a copper supplement at a different time. High amounts of fructose have the same effect. This is why we do not recommend fructose as a purified sweetener. The presence of zinc will also decrease absorption, due to the competition for absorption sites. Copper can leach from copper water pipes and holding tanks, cooking pots, and eating utensils.

Sources of copper include shellfish and legumes.

Selenium

Selenium is part of glutathione peroxidase, one of the enzyme systems responsible for defending the body from reactive oxygen species. It also helps promote the types of prostaglandins that reduce inflammation. Animal studies indicate that selenium inhibits the formation of tumors and may slow their growth. When zinc levels are low, antibody production and the activity of NK cells are decreased. There is also evidence that selenium may be directly toxic to tumors.

The DRI of selenium is 55 mcg/day. Sources of selenium include swordfish and Brazil nuts (the two most concentrated sources), salmon, tuna, lobster, shrimp, oysters, haddock, sunflower seeds, barley, brown rice, and red Swiss chard.

Chromium

Chromium is part of glucose tolerance factor, which works with insulin to see that it is absorbed and utilized by the cells. Cancer cells alter carbohydrate metabolism, causing high blood glucose levels. Chromium works to stabilize glucose levels in the blood, leaving less circulating fuel for the tumor.

Sources of chromium include whole grains and high-chromium brewer's yeast.

Mineral intake is difficult to measure. The total amount of any given mineral, calculated by adding the contribution of each component of the diet, does not accurately reflect how much of that mineral is actually going to be absorbed from a meal. Mineral absorption and utilization depend not only on how much of a mineral is present in the meal, but on the other foods present in the stomach, the acidity in the stomach, the bioavailability of the mineral, mineral interactions, length of time in the digestive tract, mineral stores in the body, and mineral needs. Mineral balance is also affected by how much is stored in the body and how much is excreted.

10

Antioxidants, Phytochemicals, and Cancer

Phytochemicals come in such a wide variety of forms and functions that they are difficult to classify. This chapter will focus only on those properties that can aid you in your treatment plan. We will look at what phytochemicals are, where they come from, and how they support the immune system, increase enzyme levels, and prevent metastasis. We will also look at antioxidants that are not vitamins or minerals.

For many years a food's nutritional value was determined by its vitamin, mineral, and energy content. The old adage of an apple a day was deemed a myth, for the lowly apple had few of these to offer. It lacked the vitamin C found in citrus fruits, the calcium found in leafy greens, and the complex carbohydrates found in potatoes. In short, it was a nutritional bust. Down to the bottom of the vegetable pile for the once proud apple.

Then fiber was "discovered." America was constipated, and this was the cure. Dubbed "nature's broom," roughage was judged necessary to keep the colon clean and tidy. The apple advanced one notch to a laxative by virtue of its fiber.

Today the new kid on the nutrition block is the phyto-chemical (*phyto* = plant). Also called nutraceuticals and anutrients, **phytochemicals** are naturally occurring plant compounds that the human body has learned to use in novel ways. They are not related to each other chemically and have no deficiency symptoms. In fact, most of them have yet to be discovered. Chemicals such as polyphenols which kill viruses, glutathione which quenches free radicals, and pectin which reduces cholesterol have suddenly become the "in" topic. And, you guessed it, all of these can be found in the apple. Back to the top of the heap again!

You can often tell how good a source of phytochemicals a food is by your eyes and nose. Pigments have antioxidant properties, with orange beta-carotene being the most familiar. Strong odors are often associated with phytochemicals such as the sulfur-containing compounds that give cabbage and the other cruciferous vegetables their distinctive aroma. Other phytochemicals are less obvious. But nature has not wasted any part of a plant. We may not understand why or how phytochemicals work, but it is an undeniable fact that whole foods promote health and prevent disease.

Let's begin with some of the larger phytochemical families.

Carotenoids

The carotenoids are a huge family of more than six hundred yellow to red pigments, of which beta-carotene is the most famous. Each carotene is unique, so different carotenes are preferred by different organs. The cells in your liver, heart, thyroid gland, kidneys, and pancreas prefer beta-carotene and lycopene equally, while the cells of the adrenal glands and testes mainly prefer just lycopene. Zeaxanthin and beta-carotene are favorites in the ovaries, whereas in the macula of the eye, lutein and zeaxanthin predominate.

The foods in Table 10.1 will supply your body with a variety of these important antioxidant pigments. Since different parts of your body prefer different carotenes, you should not take megadoses of any one. For instance, large doses of beta-carotene have been shown to decrease absorption of other important antioxidants because they compete for absorption.

Beta-carotene is the object of most research and has been shown to have antitumor effects by causing regression and redifferentiation of established cancers. However alpha-carotene can be up to ten times more effective in this manner. See Chapter 4 on the immune system for more information on these pigments.

The Flavonoids

The flavonoid group of compounds was originally referred to as "vitamin P." The P stood for "permeability

Table 10.1 Carotene Food Groups

ALPHA- AND BETA-CAROTENE

Carrots
Sweet potatoes
Pumpkin
Winter squash
Yams

BETA-CRYPTOXANTHIN

Oranges
Grapefruit
Lemons
Tangerines

ZEAXANTHIN

Peaches
Corn
Tangerines

LUTEIN AND BETA-CAROTENE

Deep green leafy vegetables

LYCOPENE

Tomatoes
Watermelon

ASTAXANTHIN

Salmon

How to Supplement Beta-Carotene

It has been shown that pure beta-carotene in amounts exceeding 20,000 IU depresses the blood-circulating levels of other, more important carotenoids. This may be due to competition for absorption.

Do take a supplement that contains a mixture of naturally occurring carotenoids. This includes but is not limited to beta- and alpha-carotene, lutein, cryptoxanthin, and lycopene.

An IU (international unit of activity) refers to the amount of vitamin A the body can make from the dose. However, most xanthophylls and lycopene do not have provitamin A activity and therefore have no IU activity. Xanthophylls and lycopene should be listed in milligrams, not in international units.

Check the color of the supplement. It should be orange to red. If not, it may contain few or no carotenoids. Or the supplement may be old and the pigments oxidized. The breakdown products of most carotenoids are colorless.

factor" (and for paprika, the source), since an extract of Hungarian peppers enhanced vitamin C's ability to repair the permeability of blood vessels found in scurvy. Today we know these citrus flavonoids are only one of many different types of flavonoids. Flavonoids are commonly referred to as bioflavonoids—meaning flavonoids with biologic activity—or just flavons.

Flavonoids, like the carotenes, are pigments. They produce a wide variety of colors in fruits and vegetables, from the colorless flavonones in citrus fruit to the red and blue anthocyanins in berries, and are usually concentrated in the peel, skin, or outer layer of the plant. Tea and wine are also sources of bioflavonoids. They appear to work synergistically with vitamin C and stimulate the detoxification of drugs by the liver enzymes.

Bioflavonoids important to cancer patients include the following:

- Quercetin is the most commonly occurring flavonoid and one of the most powerful antioxidants. It blocks the manufacture of the prostaglandin E_2 series, which can depress the immune system, and may be directly toxic to cancer cells.
- Rutin, a flavonoid found in buckwheat, may also be toxic to cancer cells. It is an important antioxidant that strengthens the capillaries.
- Aglycone, kaempferol, and myricetin are flavonoids found in green and black tea. They are responsible for the potent cancer-fighting and antioxidant properties of Japanese green tea.

Cruciferous Vegetables

The National Cancer Institute has linked cruciferous vegetables to a reduced risk of colon cancer and protective effects against cancer of the lung, esophagus, larynx, rectum, colon, repetition, stomach, prostate, and bladder. Cruciferous vegetables contain such potential cancer-preventing or cancer-inhibiting substances as aromatic isothiocyanates (benzyl isothiocyanate, phenethyl isothiocyanate), glucosinolates (glucobrassin, glucotropaeolin), flavones, indoles, and phenols. Some of these phytochemicals stop carcinogens before they have a chance to alter DNA structure. Others slow the development or spread of cancerous cells or stimulate the release of anticancer enzymes. Indoles increase the detoxification of estrogen, reducing that hormone's chance of enhancing cancer growth in hormone-sensitive cells.

These vegetables also contain the antioxidant vitamins A, C, and E, which clean up cancer-promoting free radicals and are good sources of soluble and insoluble fiber.

Seasonings

Garlic is a natural antibiotic that will help stave off bacterial and viral infections. Eating garlic after cancer treatments when immune function is low will increase protection from infections. Garlic contains organosulfur compounds (siallyl sulfide, diallyl disulfide, allyl mercaptan, allyl methyl disulfide) that block carcinogenic activation, increase carcinogenic detoxification, and block tumor growth. Other members of the allium family with similar properties include onions, leeks, and shallots. Since garlic is a potent antibiotic, it should never be taken or eaten in megadoses.

Shiitake, maitake, and reishi mushrooms contain lenitan, a biological response modifier that increases immune system response to cancer cells. Enjoy the mushrooms or supplements that are available.

Other seasonings with medicinal effects are the following:

- Rosemary contains four different antioxidants that help increase immune function.
- Ginger in fresh or powdered form is as effective as popular antinausea drugs for curbing motion sickness. Before chemotherapy starts, try it to reduce nausea.
- Peppermint stimulates bile flow and the appetite and aids digestion.
- Nutmeg can reduce peristalsis (involuntary contractions) of the gastrointestinal tract during diarrhea.

Soy Products

The consumption of soy products by people with cancer has been dubbed the "tofu treatment." As silly as it sounds, the tofu treatment really works. One cup of soybeans contains 28 grams of protein (half the RDA), fiber, zinc, B vitamins, half a day's supply of iron, and loads of highly absorbable calcium. Just on the basis of their vitamin and mineral content, soy foods are of therapeutic value. What is special about soy foods, however, is the types of phytochemicals present in them.

Soy products appear to inhibit breast cancer by decreasing the level of circulating estrogen, thereby blocking the cancer-promoting action of estrogen. One serving a day of soy may decrease the risk of developing a number of cancers by nearly 40 percent. Soy also has a cholesterol-lowering effect. Some of the phytochemicals found in soy include the following:

- Phytoesterols help protect against heart disease and are effective against skin cancer.
- Saponins are antioxidants and play a role in cancer prevention.
- Genistein, an isoflavone found in soy products, is protective against colon, breast, lung, prostate, and skin cancer and leukemia.
- Daidzein, another isoflavone, has slowed the growth of breast cancer cells in vivo.
- Protease inhibitors appear to inhibit or prevent cancer growth

Antioxidants

Antioxidants are nutrients that protect the body from damage done by oxygen free radicals (reactive oxygen species). Most of them are considered phytochemicals. There is a great deal of controversy regarding antioxidants and cancer treatment. Some researchers believe that antioxidants enhance chemo- and radiation therapy, making cancer cells more vulnerable to treatment while at the same time protecting healthy cells from the treatment's toxic effects. Other researchers believe that antioxidants can strengthen cancer cells along with the healthy cells and so should be avoided. In between are others who feel that antioxidants should be avoided during the weeks before therapy and then taken during it. The matter is further complicated by different types of cancers reacting differently to different kinds of antioxidants. Ask your oncologist how or if you should take antioxidants for your particular kind of cancer and cancer treatment.

As nutritionists we believe that your antioxidants should come from food and not out of a bottle. Study after study has shown that antioxidants are more potent and effective when consumed as part of a whole food. We do recommend a multivitamin mineral supplement that contains small amounts of many phytochemical antioxidants to supplement your diet. See Appendix A for information on ordering such supplements.

At this time we do not recommend large doses of any one nutrient. This type of treatment can be very valuable and effective for certain types of cancers but *should only* be attempted under the care of a knowledgeable physician.

One of the reasons a whole-food diet is so healthful is that it provides many phytochemicals. These substances can have a profound effect on the immune system. The best way to get these compounds is through eating a varied diet. Food pills, juice pills, and the like are only pale imitations of real foods.

DIET PLANS: DEVELOPING YOUR NUTRITIONAL THERAPY REGIME

All popular diets today are defined by their carb, protein, and fat percentages. But a diet must be more than the sum of its macronutrient levels. Weight loss is good, but your diet must also reduce inflammation by being low in animal foods and fat and rich in oily fish. It must be able to reduce oxygen damage (oxidation) by being rich in fruits, vegetables, and whole grains. It also must be easy to follow and contain enough food so you're not hungry.

The two diets in Chapters 14 and 15 are an attempt to provide the best of the high- and low-carbohydrate worlds. Many people find they get sick of the low-carb diet after a few months and quit. To help prevent this, we have increased the carbs a bit to bring in more variety. The high-carb diet is naturally low glycemic and does not have as many carbs as similar diets. The carbs that are included come packaged with lots of fiber and nutrients.

Both diet plans in this section are whole-foods diets. They are rich in antioxidants, fiber, and the monounsaturated fats that can protect your tissues from oxidative stress. They are also low in saturated fats and the arachidonic acid that can cause inflammation and high in the omega-3 fatty acids that can prevent inflammation. Both diets have a minimum of packaged and processed foods, no bakery products made with refined flour and sugar, no candy bars or other sweets, no high-fat meats or deep-fried food, and no sauces high in saturated fat. Both diets stress portion control as a way of maintaining or losing weight.

A whole-foods diet does not rely on artificial sweeteners but instead uses natural noncaloric and low-caloric sweeteners. Of course, there are times when you need to feast. Feast foods and treats always have their place, and you should never feel guilty about them. You must simply be careful that the occasional treat does not become the weekly habit.

Cancer and cancer treatments can deplete your body of nutrient stores and cause weight loss by decreasing your appetite and your body's ability to digest and absorb nutrients. At the same time, cancer speeds up the metabolic rate, increasing your need for nutrients. A balanced, supplemented diet with adequate calories and protein can provide these extra nutrients and help you to fend off weakness, repair tissue damage, boost your immune system, and generally aid in the healing process.

In addition to the two whole-foods diets, we have also provided separate nutritional recommendations for weight gain, weight loss, lactose intolerance, chemotherapy, and radiation therapy. The first diet (in Chapter 14) is a balanced low-fat (30 percent), high-carbohydrate (55 percent) diet. Because we have heard from so many patients who want to try a low-carbohydrate diet, we have included one (in Chapter 15) that contains more carbohydrates than Atkins or Zone diets but still less than the usual high-carb diets (45 percent). Both diets have sample menu plans to help you plan your meals.

When you have cancer, it can be difficult to get all the nutrients you need. It is best to make dietary changes before treatment begins so you can increase your nutrient stores and prepare your body for the friendly fire of cancer treatment (which we discuss in Chapter 11).

One warning: it is impossible to eat exactly 55 or 45 percent of calories from carbohydrates. Some days you will eat 60 percent, and some days you will eat 50 percent. When we were analyzing our two diets, we found they naturally hit the middle at 50 percent a good part of the time. Listen to your body and let it make the choice for you. If you need to lose weight, pick the diet that will decrease your hunger the most.

11

Friendly Fire: The Nutritional Side Effects of Treatment

Unlike my (Maureen's) husband, who never worries and has no nerve endings to speak of, I was and still am a weenie, a wimp, a wuss. My body does not recognize the existence of small pains: either something does not hurt at all, or it hurts terribly—usually the latter. New experiences are not something I treasure or seek voluntarily. Needles, doctors, and hospitals send my blood pressure plummeting. Needless to say, the stage was neatly set for one of the worst experiences of my life.

But it didn't happen that way. I got through it. Cancer treatment was not fun, and I certainly have no desire to repeat the experience, but I would not let it get the better of me. I took control of what I could and let go of what I couldn't. I read, I researched, I visualized, and I prayed. As the start of therapy drew near, I was petrified. I had heard all of the usual horror stories; so have you, I'm sure. But the chemotherapy was not as bad as I had imagined, and the surgery was uncomfortable but not painful.

The first two courses of chemotherapy were the worst. The methotrexate caused a loss of hair, very painful sores on my tongue, a sore throat, pustules on my forehead, nausea, fatigue, and headaches. But I got myself a wig, stuffed my mouth with Xylocaine-saturated cotton, and taught my Irish dance classes by holding up signs. I slicked my hair over the pustules and danced in a show myself that St. Patrick's Day. The next two courses seemed easier to me but were actually harder on my body. The actinomycin seemed only to cause fatigue, but both courses of it ended early because of liver damage. And I still continued to teach dancing while trying to dodge the four-year-old twins, who always attempted to yank off my wig. While you may not feel like dancing a jig during your treatment, it does help to stay on your regular routine as much as possible.

You are probably familiar with the old axiom, "You are what you eat." But the opposite is also true: "You eat what you are." When you are feeling poorly from cancer treatments or the cancer itself, your diet is also apt to be poor. When I was in treatment, I had a very active toddler, and getting my husband and son fed often took up most of my energy. I put my needs last. If you are doing the same, this has to change. If you have young children, discuss sharing cooking responsibilities with your spouse. Older children and teens can be pressed into service to help feed younger ones. The job of the digestive system is to take in nutrients that the immune system needs, but your main job now is getting nutritious food into your stomach.

Treatment and the cancer itself can make eating a challenge. Patients must deal with side effects such as nausea, dry mouth, and oral and esophageal mucositis. Other side effects that can cause malnutrition include the following:

- Altered taste and smell. Tumor growth, radiation, and chemotherapy treatments all have the potential to alter the ability to taste and smell. Foods may taste bitter or metallic. This change may lead to appetite loss, which in turn reduces nutrient intake, resulting in weight loss and ultimately malnutrition.
- Anorexia. A number of treatment side effects—loss of taste, nausea, diarrhea, and vomiting—can cause loss of appetite. Even though it may be difficult, try to eat as much as you can. Remember, if you do not use your gut, you will lose your gut. Malnutrition will decrease the amount of digestive enzymes available and decrease the absorptive area of the small intestine even when food is digested.
- Blood sugar disorders. Stabilizing blood sugar is critical in controlling cancer. High blood sugar levels (hyperglycemia) and low blood sugar levels (hypoglycemia) stress the immune system, weakening your ability to heal. Cancer cells need glucose for fuel and will alter the body's metabolism to keep blood sugar levels high. Starve your tumor by eliminating refined dietary sugars and increasing fiber.
- Food allergens. Avoid food allergens, as food allergies may be exacerbated by cancer treatments. Eat a variety of foods to avoid developing a sensitivity to any particular food.

- Malabsorption. Food may not be absorbed properly through the intestines into the bloodstream. For example, each segment of the intestines absorbs different nutrients. Surgery to remove part of the intestine dramatically affects the body's ability to absorb the corresponding nutrients. Pancreatic cancer can cause a decrease in insulin production, affecting carbohydrate metabolism. Radiation or surgery of the intestines or other areas of the abdomen can cause diarrhea, cramps, or decreased absorption.
- Maldigestion. The body's ability to produce digestive enzymes and break down foods for absorption may be reduced by the stress of illness. Signals that normally stimulate your appetite may not be functioning. This can prevent the stomach from releasing digestive juices.
- Difficulty swallowing. Difficulty in chewing and swallowing may be the result of tumors in the head or neck area or an aftereffect of surgery.
- Weight loss cycle. Decreased appetite and the resulting weight loss can lead to fatigue and depression. This, in turn, leads to less activity and even more weight loss. Soon the body's resistance to disease and ability to heal decline as well. Lower resistance may affect the amount of chemotherapy or radiation treatment that can be delivered, hindering your healing process.

This chapter shows how nutrition therapy can help you cope with some of the most difficult side effects of treatment.

Nausea and Vomiting

One of the most common side effects of cancer treatment is gastrointestinal upset. Most of the time this condition is minor and does not last long. In many cases, the nausea and vomiting disappear when the treatment is stopped. In severe or prolonged cases, it is necessary to take an anti-emetic drug so that the body is able to get the nutrients it needs. Although some people may balk at taking yet another drug, good nutrition at this point is more important.

Vomiting is how the body gets rid of food that should not be in the stomach. It is stimulated by sensory receptors in the wall of the stomach (Figure 11.1), including

Figure 11.1 Locations of sensors that trigger vomiting

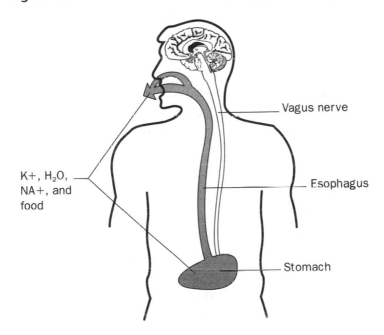

K+, H₂O, NA+, and food

Vagus nerve

Esophagus

Stomach

stretch receptors that indicate when the stomach is too full and chemoreceptors that detect possible toxins and poisons. The emetic center in the brain responds to these signals as well as to the presence of possible toxic substances in the blood by causing a wave of reverse peristalsis to expel the contents.

While vomiting is unpleasant and even painful when coupled with a raw throat and mouth sores, it is only dangerous when it is severe or prolonged. The main danger is loss of fluids and electrolytes from the body, causing dehydration, weight loss, and an electrolyte imbalance. You can quickly become dehydrated from vomiting; and after two days, the dehydration may be severe. Intravenous fluids may be needed to rehydrate your tissues and reverse the imbalances.

Cancer therapy has changed greatly since I had chemotherapy. A friend who was recently treated for colon cancer was able to get her chemotherapy from a pump she wore. This allowed a smaller dose of the drug, and she had far fewer side effects than I experienced. As science progresses we can expect cancer treatment to become easier and less toxic to our bodies. Until then, however, we need to deal with the side effects that remain.

Causes of nausea include the following:

- Chemotherapy. The most common side effect from chemotherapy is nausea and vomiting. Chemotherapy causes nausea by acting on both the brain and stomach. The emetic center in the brain that controls vomiting may be stimulated by the drugs. Some drugs work on the stomach itself, causing local irritation that results in upset.

- Stress. The stress from fear, pain, or phobias (e.g., of needles, hospitals, blood) is often overlooked as a cause of stomach upset. For some of us, the first sign of stress is an upset stomach.
- Radiation. Radiation of the spine and skull for central nervous system tumors often causes nausea. Radiation treatment to the gastrointestinal tract will also cause upset soon after administration, as can total body irradiation conditioning for bone marrow transplant.

Words to Know

Nausea: Upset stomach.

Anticipatory nausea: An upset stomach before treatment caused by the thought of treatment or even the sight of the hospital or clinic where treatment is given.

Emesis: Vomiting.

Emetic center: The area of the brain that controls vomiting.

Antiemetics: Drugs that reduce nausea and vomiting.

Emetogenic potential: The ability of a drug to cause nausea and vomiting. Drugs such as cisplatin, dacarbazine, and mechlorethamine have a high emetogenic potential, since they cause nausea and vomiting in more than 90 percent of patients.

Food aversions: A phenomenon in which foods eaten close to the time of a nausea-causing treatment become linked in the brain with the symptoms caused by a treatment. Aromatic foods are at greatest risk for this.

Guidelines for Dealing with Nausea and Vomiting

During treatment, it's also possible to acquire learned food aversions. Immediately after my first chemotherapy treatment, I went to a luncheon where freshly grated horseradish was served with corned beef. I was nauseated at the time, and the back of my hand hurt from the IV. For ten years, every time I smelled horseradish or corned beef, I would get nauseated and the back of my hand would hurt. This reaction is not at all uncommon. To prevent it from destroying the enjoyment of your favorite foods, do not eat them immediately before or after treatments. Not all of these suggestions will work for every person. Sometimes the best thing to do is listen to the wisdom of your body and eat whatever nutritious food you can tolerate or enjoy.

It's important to plan ahead. Think out of the box. Get ready to combat the problem with these tactics before treatment:

- Ask your physician about the emetic potential of your treatment plan and the advisability of an anti-emetic drug. The drug must be taken before treatment begins if it is to be effective.
- If stress first manifests itself in your stomach or if you are phobic of hospitals, needles, blood, or IVs, be prepared for stress-induced nausea. The only way I was able to overcome a phobia of needles to start methotrexate injections was to see a medical hypnotist. The result was stress-free injections and a stomach that was free of knots.

- Arrange for someone else to prepare your food. If that is not possible, prepare foods ahead of time. Pack foods into single-serving bags that are ready to eat when you are.
- Prepare ahead for dehydration by stocking an electrolyte replacement. Avoid sport drinks that contain sugar; they can make vomiting worse. We suggest a product like ElectroMIX (alacer.com) that contains only electrolytes with no sugar or artificial sweeteners.
- A few hours before treatment, place an acupressure band around your wrist. These bands stimulate the acupressure point that relieves nausea. They are available in most drugstores and pharmacies.
- If you react to stress with stomach butterflies, remember to breathe from your abdomen deeply and slowly. It's amazing how many people forget to breathe during stressful situations.
- If your chemotherapy is being given in a single daily dose as opposed to over five days via a pump, do not eat for two hours before or after a treatment. The drugs can stimulate the stomach and emetic center in the brain to produce nausea.
- Avoid eating highly flavored or aromatic foods on the day of your treatment or during that week. When eaten again, they can cause a "nausea flashback."

To *prevent* nausea during and after treatment, follow these suggestions:

- During the week of your treatment eat small, frequent meals rather than three large ones each day, and do not drink large amounts of liquids with your meals. Too much food or liquid can overexpand the stomach, activating the stretch receptors and stimulating the emetic center. For the same reason, do not drink carbonated or fizzy beverages.

- Position is important. Sit up to eat and do not lie down immediately afterward. A prone position can cause the food to back up into the esophagus.
- Make mealtimes calm and relaxing. Read or watch TV while eating. Rest and relax (in a sitting position) after eating. Avoid arguments or confrontations during mealtimes.
- Avoid cooking odors. Strong food aromas can be reduced by using a pressure cooker to prepare family meals. Odor neutralizers are handy to keep around. These products remove smells instead of masking them with a perfumy odor. They come in spray bottles and are often marketed as pet odor removers.
- Heavy perfumes and smoke odors can also provoke nausea. Buy cleaning products and personal care items that are marked as unscented or fragrance free. (The perfumy odor of fabric softener sheets in the clothes dryer used to make me nauseous.)
- Do not eat greasy or high-fat foods. Fat causes food to remain in the stomach longer, increasing the chance that you may vomit. Avoid all deep-fried foods, meat, whole milk and cheeses, butter, oils, salad dressings, potato and corn chips, and nut butters, including peanut butter and tahini.
- Eat foods that are easy to digest, such as crackers, lightly salted pretzels, dry toast, and soft bread.

Avoid raw or highly fibrous foods, and chew each mouthful thoroughly. Later in the day eat a low-fat, high-protein food such as skinless chicken breast, mild fish, or a legume soup.

- Avoid foods with strong odors or flavors, such as onions, garlic, horseradish, cabbage, broccoli, cauliflower, brussels sprouts and other members of the cruciferous family, eggs, hot peppers, and any other highly spiced foods. Avoid any food that "repeats" on you.
- Avoid drinks that are full of sugar. High-sugar drinks remain in the stomach longer than low-sugar drinks and can cause nausea.

To *relieve* nausea after treatment, follow these guidelines:

- Cold, nonacidic liquids often help to settle a stomach. This includes small sips of ice water, ice chips, iced herbal teas, iced tea, and small tastes of all-fruit sorbets.
- Clear or salty liquids are easy to keep down. Miso soup and broths are nutritious choices. Peppermint tea calms some stomachs.
- If you do not feel like eating, don't. Listen to your stomach, and wait until the nausea passes.
- Ginger capsules will often help to relieve nausea but will not work once you have started to vomit.
- Place an ice pack on the back of your neck. Keep a supply of gel pacs in the freezer for quick use.
- Open some windows and let in fresh, cool air. Stuffy, stale, or smoky air will make nausea worse and increase the chance of vomiting.

- Keep your teeth and tongue clean, brushed, and flossed and your mouth rinsed. This will help keep bad flavors and odors from developing.

If you are dealing with severe nausea and the suggestions listed here do not work, call your doctor or nurse. You may need IV hydration and electrolytes.

Dry Mouth and Difficulty Swallowing

During treatment, many patients experience dry mouth, which makes chewing and swallowing food difficult. Causes of dry mouth include the following:

- Chemotherapy. Some chemotherapeutic agents such as bleomycin and dactinomycin cause a temporary dryness of the mouth. Antinausea drugs may also have this effect.
- Radiation. Radiation to the neck or head may cause damage to the salivary glands. This may result in a decrease in the amount of saliva or in the quality of the saliva, making it thick or viscous.
- Surgery. Surgery to the head or neck that removes one or more of the salivary glands will reduce secretions according to the extent of the surgery.

Since saliva keeps the mouth clean, a dry mouth can become a breeding ground for bacteria, which can promote tooth decay and cause infections. You depend on your teeth and gums to prepare the food you eat for digestion. When they are diseased or painful, good nutrition

---

Words to Know

Xerostomia: A decrease in saliva that causes the sensation of a dry mouth.

Dysphagia: Difficulty in swallowing.

Salivary glands: The glands that secrete saliva, including the large parotid, submaxillary, and sublingual glands.

Saliva: A mixture of secretions from the salivary and oral mucous glands that keeps the tissues of the mouth moist and lubricates food to facilitate swallowing.

Sialagogue: A drug or other agent that increases the flow of saliva.

---

becomes difficult. Since many cancer treatments will cause soreness or pain to the tissues of the mouth, gums, and throat, these structures must be in good condition to start with. Good oral hygiene is necessary to prevent pain when the immune system is depressed due to treatment. Before starting your cancer treatment program, start a program of oral health to protect your mouth from developing infections that can undermine your treatment and the ability of your body to heal.

Guidelines for Dealing with Dry Mouth and Difficulty Swallowing

Before meals, tart tastes will stimulate salivary flow. Add a tablespoon of fresh or frozen lemon juice to a small glass of water. Drink it fifteen minutes before mealtime.

Use these pointers during meals:

- Eat smaller, more frequent meals instead of three large ones.
- Avoid dry or sticky foods such as crackers, bread, or nut butters.
- Take small sips of water as you chew. This makes the food easier to swallow.
- Do not try to chew large pieces of food. Cut food into bite-sized pieces that are easier to swallow.
- Eat moist foods such as casseroles, stews, soups, fruits, and liquids.
- Add extra sauces, gravies, and broth to foods.
- Add vinegar, pickles, or lemon juice to food to stimulate saliva.

Between meals, follow these guidelines:

- Keep a small water bottle with you and take frequent sips. My favorite is a slim plastic bottle with a pop-up top that held a "designer" water. The water was gone quickly, but the bottle has lasted for months. Carry your bottle with you in your purse, coat, or briefcase. Keep water at your bedside for when you wake up with that "cottony" feeling.
- Suck on ice cubes or ice chips when they are available.
- A dry mouth is a haven for bacteria that can cause tooth decay or tissue infections. Keep teeth and tongue brushed and flossed and mouth tissues rinsed.
- Use a wetting agent for the mouth such as Salivart or Xero-lube. These can be purchased in drugstores and pharmacies.

Guidelines for Oral Hygiene and Health

Before cancer treatment, see your dentist for a pretreatment evaluation. If you have any difficulty eating because of your teeth, now is the time to have cavities filled and other dental work done. In addition, be sure to do the following:

- Inform your dentist about your health problems. Extraction and other oral surgeries must be done at least a month in advance of cancer therapy to give oral tissues time to heal. Once therapy begins, healing and tissue regeneration will stop. This can result in permanent dental problems.
- Make sure that your dentist and/or oral surgeon has the contact information for your oncologist and family doctor and an up-to-date list of all the medications and supplements that you use.
- Have your teeth cleaned. A clean mouth will give bacteria and fungi no place to hide and feed.
- If you wear dentures, make sure that they fit properly without causing any irritations.

Once treatment begins, follow a strict dental health regime at home:

- Brush your teeth gently, three times a day, with a soft-bristle toothbrush. Use a nonabrasive fluoride toothpaste.
- Floss teeth every day to remove trapped food and tartar.
- If your gums become too sore to brush, clean around gums with a soft cloth. Use a nonirritating

toothpaste. A paste of baking soda and water makes a gentle but refreshing cleaner.

- Avoid mouthwashes that contain alcohol. They can irritate tissues.
- Rinse your mouth with water after drinking or eating sweet foods or juices.
- Mouth irritations and sores can be relieved by the topical application of vitamin E or tea tree oil.
- Make sure your toothbrush does not become a breeding place for germs. Replace it often, and always rinse it well and leave to air-dry before putting it away.

Taste Alterations

Stimulation of the taste buds results in four taste sensations: sweet, sour, bitter, and salty. The brain decides on the type of taste by the degree of stimulation of these four sensations. All flavors are a combination of these taste bud sensations combined with sensations received by the olfactory (odor) receptors and the trigeminal nerves, which detect irritants such as hot peppers and mint. Since the taste buds are formed from fast-dividing epithelial tissue, they are particularly sensitive to cancer therapies.

Causes of taste alterations include the following:

- Chemotherapy. Taste alterations are associated with certain chemotherapeutic drugs. Cisplatin, 5-fluorouracil, dactinomycin, daunorubicin, and methotrexate are associated with taste alterations. Cyclophosphamide and vincristine may be tasted after injection. Any chemotherapeutic drug can cause a bitter or metallic taste in some people.

- Radiation therapy. Radiation can injure or kill taste buds. Radiation to the head and neck causes a temporary loss of taste two to three weeks after treatment. It can last for several weeks. Total body irradiation in preparation for a bone marrow transplant also causes injury. The taste buds recover forty-five to sixty days after transplantation.
- Surgery. Surgical removal of parts of the mouth that perceive taste will cause a permanent loss of those taste receptors. Sweet and salty sensations are eliminated after removal of the tongue. Removal of the palate results in the loss of most sour and bitter receptor sites.
- Anesthesia. Sometimes anesthetics administered for surgery can result in a temporary loss of taste. This can last up to sixty days, but taste evenutally returns.
- Infection. Oral infections that cause inflammation of the mucous membranes (mucositis) may decrease taste sensations, since the taste receptor cells become inflamed.

Guidelines for Dealing with Taste Alterations

When you find it difficult to eat for any reason, you must make every meal and every food count. Now is not the

---

Words to Know

Dysgeusia: A change in the sense of taste.
Hypogeusia: A decrease in the ability to taste.
Ageusia: Complete loss of the ability to taste.
Taste buds: Chemical receptors for the taste nerve fibers.
Mucositis: An inflammation of the mucous membranes, causing mouth sores.

---

time to abandon good food habits. Although you can get needed calories from ice cream, there are ways to get sufficient calories without resorting to junk food. The sensation of taste is a nutritional factor that is often overlooked. Taste changes are not life-threatening complications, but they can make good nutrition more difficult. Taste triggers the salivary glands necessary for proper chewing and swallowing and stimulates the flow of the gastric juices necessary for digestion. Loss of taste means a decrease in the pleasure found in eating, which can cause a decrease in appetite.

Use these pointers before a chemotherapy treatment:

- Do not eat favorite foods before chemotherapy. The changes in taste may cause an unpleasant association with the food. Snack on crackers or unsalted pretzels instead.
- If chemotherapy causes a bad taste in your mouth, suck on a lemon drop or peppermint candy during treatment.

After treatment or surgery or during your week of treatment, follow these guidelines:

- If you develop a low threshold for bitter tastes, avoid beef (yet another reason!). Substitute skinless white poultry, mild-tasting fish, soy foods, nut butters, and legumes for protein sources.
- Depending on your tolerance, either increase or decrease the amount of salt in food.
- Use herbs, spices, flavor extracts, and marinades to increase the flavor of food. If the tissues of the mouth are inflamed, avoid any hot spices that may irritate sore membranes.
- Foods that are cold or at room temperature may be more palatable than hot ones.
- Appeal to your other senses to make up for your lack of taste. Use highly aromatic foods, such as garlic and onions, and foods with a variety of colors and textures.
- Unpleasant food odors may be confused with unpleasant tastes. See the section on nausea for tips on how to avoid them.
- Use plastic eating utensils instead of metallic ones.
- Drink filtered water. Carafe-type water purifiers are inexpensive and greatly reduce the chemical flavors and odors common in tap water.
- A zinc supplement may increase taste sensitivity. Ask your physician.
- Keep your mouth, tongue, and teeth clean and well rinsed to wash away bad tastes.

Anorexia

Do not confuse the anorexia some patients experience with anorexia nervosa, an eating disorder unrelated to cancer. Rather, early satiety may kill the appetite, making proper nutrition difficult to achieve. Loss of appetite results in weight loss, malnutrition, and decreased immunity to infections.

Anorexia does not have a single cause. It is the result of a number of factors:

- Toxic effects of therapy. Side effects of treatment such as nausea, sore mouth and throat, stomach cramps, and taste changes can all decrease the desire to eat.
- Localized effects of the tumor. Tumors in the gastrointestinal tract that cause blockages can decrease appetite. Some tumors produce chemicals that affect the endocrine system, resulting in early satiety.

Words to Know

Anorexia: Loss of appetite or the desire to eat.

Cachexia: Loss of weight, fat, and muscle mass in patients who are eating adequate calories.

Satiety: The feeling of being full after a meal.

Early satiety: The feeling of fullness and loss of appetite after a small amount of food.

Bloating: A feeling of fullness.

- Surgery. Surgical removal of any part of the gastrointestinal tract can decrease the ability and desire to eat.

Guidelines for Dealing with Anorexia

The following solutions apply to meal planning:

- Appetite is usually best first thing in the morning, so plan to have your largest meal of the day at breakfast.
- Plan your meals and go shopping for the food yourself, if you are able.
- Eat six small meals a day instead of three large ones. Or take small bites of nutrient-dense foods every hour or so.
- Eat whenever you are hungry. Do not wait for mealtime.
- Keep cooking odors to a minimum.

When you eat, follow these hints:

- Liquid meals are often more appealing than solid ones. Drink fresh vegetable and fruit juices instead eating of whole vegetables and fruits, and drink soy milk rather than eat soybeans. Make smoothies with soft fruits such as bananas, and add a protein source such as whey.
- Do not drink liquids with meals. Eat the most nutrient-dense foods in the meal first.

- Avoid low-calorie, low-protein foods and beverages such as tea, coffee, or soda. Beverages with a high percentage of water will kill your appetite and fill you up without providing calories or protein.
- Avoid raw vegetables. Puree steamed veggies and mix them with high-calorie foods.
- Add medium-chain triglycerides, Enova oil, olive oil, canola oil, or high oleic safflower oil to foods to increase the fat content.

The following ideas may help you improve a poor appetite:

- Canned food supplements, which can be purchased at the drugstore, are a handy source of balanced nutrition in a pinch.
- Light exercise may stimulate the appetite. Ask your doctor about taking easy walks before meals.
- Create a relaxed eating atmosphere. Try enhancing your surroundings to make mealtime more appealing. Try candlelight, soft music, or a colorful table setting.
- Very sweet or tart foods may stimulate saliva. Suck on lemon wedges or try lemonade.

Oral and Esophageal Mucositis

Mucositis begins with the tissues feeling dry and looking red. The mouth and throat are sore. This is followed by swelling, ulcerations, and, in some severe cases, bleeding. This inflammation is painful and limits food intake and enjoyment. Talking becomes difficult, and a headache often accompanies the mouth pain. Because of the open sores, there is a chance for infection.

Causes of mucositis include the following:

- Chemotherapy. Treatment prevents the division of the rapidly dividing mucous membrane cells of the tongue, cheek, lips, gums, and palate, as well as the floor of the mouth and esophagus. When the top layers of cells are shed, they are not replaced. This causes inflammation as early as three days after treatment, which can progress into ulcerations after a week. Among the chemotherapeutic drugs that cause the most severe mucositis are dactinomycin, plicamycin, methotrexate, and 5-fluorouracil.
- Radiation. Radiotherapy to the head and neck can cause damage to the mucous membranes of the mouth and throat. Inflammation begins about two weeks after therapy begins and starts to heal two weeks after it ends. Radiation therapy to the thorax

---

Words to Know

Mucositis: An inflammation of the mucous membrane lining of the mouth and esophagus.

Stomatitis: An inflammation of the oral cavity.

Ulcer: An inflamed, open sore on the mucous membranes.

Esophagitis: An inflammation of the lining of the esophagus.

Dysphagia: Difficulty swallowing.

can cause inflammation to the esophagus and difficulty in swallowing.

- Total body irradiation. The preparation for bone marrow transplant is also a major cause of inflammation and ulcerations in the mouth and esophagus. This can develop as soon as four days after preparative chemotherapy and heals with marrow engraftment and the return of neutrophils.

Guidelines for Dealing with Oral and Esophageal Mucositis

For meals, follow these guidelines:

- Eat soft, nonirritating foods such as nonfat yogurt; oatmeal; brown rice farina; quinoa and other soft, well-cooked whole grains; pureed vegetables; and mashed potatoes and yams.
- Serve foods lukewarm or cold—never hot—to avoid burning already irritated tissue.
- Vegetable soups are easy on sore throats. If the pain is very severe, the soup can be processed in a blender to liquefy solids.
- Avoid acidic, tart, or spicy foods such as citrus and tomato juices and fruits, vinegar-based salad dressings and condiments, hot peppers, curry, chili, and pepper-containing condiments and seasonings. Do not drink alcohol.
- Avoid dry, rough foods such as granola and toast.
- Drink your raw vegetables by making a glass or two of fresh juice from nonacidic vegetables such as carrots, celery, and apples.

- If sores are confined to the tongue, use a straw to bypass them.
- For severe dysphagia and pain in swallowing, you may need to follow a liquid diet.

Use these pointers to heal and soothe tissues:

- Bite open a 400-IU capsule of vitamin E and swish it around your mouth before swallowing.
- Follow the recommendations for vitamin C supplementation in Chapter 8. It will help with tissue healing.
- Apply tea tree oil directly to the sores. Tea tree oil (from the tree that produces tea leaves) acts as a topical antibiotic.
- Sucking on ice chips can soothe a sore throat and help numb mouth sores.
- Keep your mouth very clean. Even though it may hurt to brush your teeth, a neglected mouth is a breeding ground for bacteria that can enter your body though the sores.
- If pain is severe enough to prevent you from eating, call your doctor or nurse. Your doctor can prescribe a local anesthetic to numb ulcers and sore spots so that you can eat.

Constipation and Diarrhea

Two colon-related problems that may affect people undergoing treatment for cancer are constipation and diarrhea.

Fortunately, nutrition therapy offers remedies for both conditions.

Digestion takes place in the alimentary canal—a thirty-foot tube that runs through the center of your body. The purpose of the digestive system is not only digestion, but absorption of what is digested, storage of what is not, and excretion of waste products and undigested food (Figure 11.2). Food moves through the alimentary canal propelled by a series of muscle contractions called peristalsis.

What causes an increase in peristalsis in one part of the alimentary canal often causes the same reaction in other parts. Let's say you are taking a drug that relaxes the muscles in your colon as a side effect. That can cause consti-

Figure 11.2 Absorption and secretion in the alimentary canal

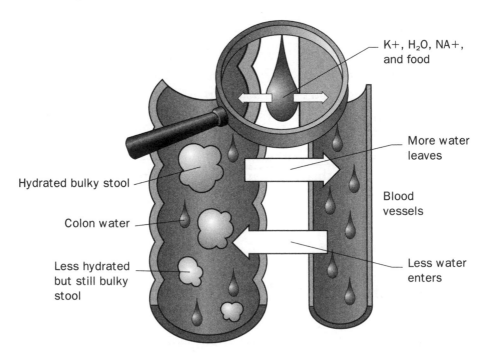

pation. But it can also cause heartburn because the muscle that keeps digestive juice in the stomach also relaxes, causing a burning splash.

The large colon is divided into four parts: the ascending, transverse, descending, and sigmoid segments. The ascending colon receives the watery chyme with undigested fiber from the small intestine. Together with the transverse colon, it reabsorbs electrolytes and water at the rate of 2 liters per day. How fast the chyme moves through these sections determines its water content. If the chyme moves too slowly, more water is absorbed and the feces are very dry, resulting in constipation (Figure 11.3). If it

Figure 11.3 Constipation

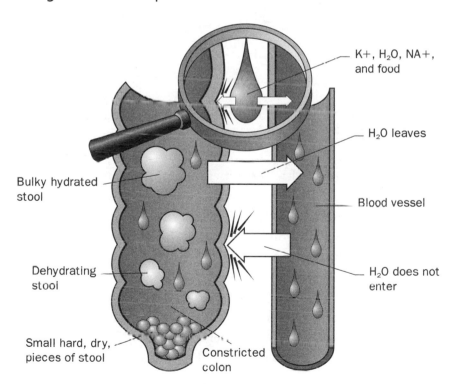

K+, H$_2$O, NA+, and food

H$_2$O leaves

Bulky hydrated stool

Blood vessel

Dehydrating stool

H$_2$O does not enter

Small hard, dry, pieces of stool

Constricted colon

Figure 11.4 Diarrhea

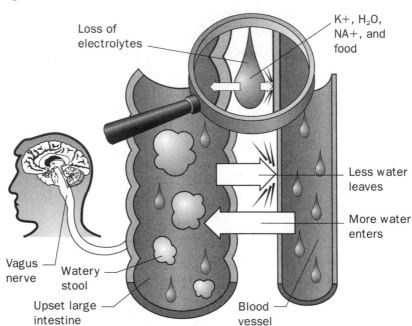

moves too fast, the water does not have time to be reabsorbed and the feces are too watery, resulting in diarrhea (Figure 11.4).

As the peristaltic movements of the colon move the dehydrating mass along, water is trapped by the undigested (primarily insoluble) fiber in the chyme, preventing the stool from becoming too dry. Other undigested (primarily soluble) fibers are eaten by the many species of "friendly" bacteria that live in the colon, causing a population explosion that contributes more bulk to the dehydrated feces. The descending and sigmoid colons are used for storage. When fecal matter is pushed into the rectum, the distention stimulates the reflex to defecate.

Guidelines for Dealing with Constipation

Causes of constipation include the following:

- Treatment side effects. The toxic effects of chemotherapy, radiation, and surgery can cause problems
  such as sore or dry mouth and throat, difficulty swallowing, nausea and vomiting, and lack of appetite.
  These side effects often greatly reduce the amount of
  fibrous foods you want to eat, causing constipation.
- Medication. The drugs used to treat side effects may
  cause constipation. For example, opioid painkillers
  can reduce peristalsis, as can the anticholinergic
  drugs used to treat vomiting and diarrhea. If you
  take any kind of opioid such as morphine or oxy-
  codon on a regular basis, you must be on some kind
  of bowel program to prevent constipation and the
  risk of developing an impaction in your colon.
- Decrease in activity. Cancer treatment often leaves a
  person feeling drained and tired. Exercise becomes
  a low priority, and all of the muscles in the body
  suffer, including those responsible for colonic
  movement.
- Stress. This causes the "fight-or-flight" response.
  The body thinks it is under attack and prepares itself
  for hard physical exertion. Organ systems not
  needed for immediate use, including the digestive
  system, are temporarily shut down, and excess bag-
  gage is cast aside. In the case of the gastrointestinal
  tract, the stomach empties itself by vomiting and
  the colon by diarrhea. Food in the small intestine
  that cannot be expelled is held until normal functioning returns.

- Loss of nerve function in the colonic muscles. Radiation and surgery can sometimes result in a temporary or permanent loss of muscle tone due to nerve damage.

The following dietary suggestions can help prevent or cure constipation:

- Wheat bran is the usual recommendation for increasing fiber intake, but rice bran tastes and works better. Sprinkle wheat bran, rice bran or polish, or ground psyllium seed on cooked or cold breakfast cereals, nonfat yogurt, or fresh fruit. Start with a teaspoon and gradually work up to a tablespoon. These foods are concentrated sources of insoluble fiber, which will increase the bulk and frequency of bowel movements by attracting water into the feces. Wheat bran holds three times its weight in water, and rice bran may hold even more. Soluble bran such as oat bran also may be effective.
- Increase the amount of water you are drinking to at least eight glasses a day. This is particularly important if you are supplementing with brans. Measure out the water in the morning so you will know how much you need to drink.
- Increase dietary fiber. Substitute whole grains for refined grains, including brown rice for white rice and whole-grain bread for white bread. Eat a variety of grains, including oats, barley, and quinoa. Each grain has its own unique blend of fibers with unique advantages. The bran in these grains is also an important source of valuable minerals. Grainwise, brown is always better.

- Increase the amount of raw vegetables you eat. Take small bites and chew them thoroughly. If chewing is a problem, grate or blend raw veggies.
- Eat more vegetables in the cabbage family, including bok choy, brussels sprouts, cauliflower, collards, and broccoli, and in the legume family, including beans and lentils. The gas they produce will help to increase the volume and softness of bowel movements.
- Nuts and seeds are not only high in fiber, they are also rich sources of healthy fats. If you need to increase calories and fiber, eat at least two servings a day. Nuts can be whole or ground into nut butters (easy to eat if you have a sore mouth or throat). Pass on the salted or oil-roasted varieties. Nuts fresh from the shell are always best.
- Add laxative foods to your diet. Prunes and prune juice are good sources of sorbitol, a natural laxative, as are apple and pear juice.
- One cup of coffee in the morning may act as a laxative, but too much can overstimulate the muscles of the colon, leaving them sluggish.
- Eliminate milk and cheese. These foods can cause constipation in some individuals.
- Drink hot or warm liquids before a meal to stimulate gastrointestinal tract movement.

The following home remedies may also help:

- Moving the external muscles of your body is one way to stimulate the muscles inside. Ask your doctor or nurse which kind of exercise is best for you. Even a short walk can be helpful.

- Laughing not only stimulates abdominal muscles but also increases endorphins, the feel-good chemicals in the brain.
- Massage your abdominal muscles.

Guidelines for Dealing with Diarrhea

Causes of diarrhea include the following:

- Chemotherapy. Chemotherapy sometimes has a toxic effect on the lining of the small intestine. Some chemotherapeutic drugs can injure the villi, preventing absorption of some nutrients, and they can damage the microvilli, decreasing the amount of enzymes produced for digestion. In the large intestine some drugs increase the rate of peristalsis and the transit time through the colon, resulting in less time for water to be reabsorbed.
- Radiation. Radiation directed to any part of the intestinal tract can cause damage to the villi of the small intestine and a decrease in repair and replacement of the injured cells. This results in loss of digestive enzymes, causing undigested food to move into the colon where it encourages diarrhea.

Words to Know

Diarrhea: Watery stools.
Peristalsis: Muscular contractions of the gastrointestinal tract that move food along.
Enteritis: Inflammation of the lining of the intestines.

- Diet. A change in diet can cause loose stools, and some foods are notorious for this ability. A temporary intolerance to milk sugar can cause diarrhea, as can some antacids.

Avoid the following foods, which may aggravate diarrhea:

- Hot foods stimulate muscle movement and may increase diarrhea. Try foods and beverages that are cold or at room temperature.
- Milk and other dairy products can cause diarrhea due to a temporary absence of lactase, the enzyme that digests lactose (milk sugar). Take lactase in pill form (available at your pharmacy or local health food store) before eating. Or follow the lactose-free diet described in Chapter 17.
- Avoid raw foods. Steam or pressure-cook vegetables.
- Avoid irritating foods such as coffee, alcohol, sweets, carbonated drinks, and highly spiced foods.
- Calorie-free carbonated drinks are not good sources of liquids, since they contain no energy sources or minerals to replace those in lost fluids. Sports drinks and fruit juices contain too much sugar, which can aggravate diarrhea.
- Avoid prunes and prune juice, apple juice, and pear juice. They all can have a laxative effect.
- Avoid foods that contain sorbitol, a natural laxative, including sugar-free and dietetic candies.
- Avoid foods that cause gas and are not well absorbed, such as beans and vegetables of the cabbage family (broccoli, cauliflower, kale, cabbage, and so on).

The following recommendations can help you choose foods to eat when you have diarrhea:

- Drink or eat starchy liquids such as a low-sodium split-pea or potato soup, rice or oat porridge, and mashed ripe bananas.
- The recommendation for diarrhea used to be a clear diet to rest the bowel. However, we now know that, instead of resting the bowel, this advice starves the bowel and therefore the body. Especially during treatment, the body needs nutrients to counteract the effects of the treatment and keep the body fighting the cancer. Stimulation from food is necessary to keep the colon working. Disuse will cause your villi to atrophy.
- Soy protein may protect against chemotherapy-induced diarrhea. Protein powders that contain only soy protein and soy milk are convenient forms of soy protein.
- Eat a cup of nonfat yogurt. It is a natural source of friendly bacteria and a natural antibiotic. Make sure that the yogurt contains live cultures. This will be stated on the container.
- Nutmeg reduces peristalsis. Add a liberal sprinkle to a cup of yogurt or a mashed banana.
- To replenish lost potassium, eat more bananas and potatoes and other high-potassium foods.

12

Prediet Preparation

This chapter will help you to prepare for your new way of eating. Before beginning your individual diet plan, it's important to have an understanding of the various food groups. We'll give you serving sizes, suggestions, and preparation tips for the foods that will add nutritional therapy to your treatment plan.

In addition, we will give you some preparation tips to make eating a pleasure while you are beginning treatment. If you are already in treatment and are short on energy or patience, pass this work on to your spouse, friends, or family as a constructive way to show their concern.

Starchy Foods
Legumes

Beans, peas, and lentils contain complex carbohydrates for pure food energy and are the perfect high-fiber, low-fat protein food. The slowly metabolized carbohydrates

Table 12.1 Types of Legumes

Soybeans	Fava beans
Adzuki beans	Kidney beans
Lima beans	Navy beans
Black beans	White beans
Black-eyed peas	Chickpeas
Brown beans	Lentils (red, yellow, and brown)
Pinto beans	
Red beans	Split and green peas

release glucose gradually into the bloodstream, which makes them the ideal food for stabilizing blood sugar. These foods also contain compounds called **protease inhibitors**, which may inhibit tumor growth. The fiber binds with toxins in the colon and carries them out before they can be reabsorbed.

Legumes (Table 12.1) are excellent sources of protein. One cup of soybeans contains 28 grams of protein (half the DRI), fiber, zinc, B vitamins, half a day's supply of iron, and loads of highly absorbable calcium.

Here are some preparation tips for cooking with legumes:

- Dried legumes can take a long time to cook and usually require soaking overnight and cooking for 1 hour or more, depending on the type of bean. A pressure cooker allows you to skip the overnight soak and shortens the cooking time to about 30 minutes.
- Beano contains a digestive enzyme that eliminates the flatulent effects of beans and gas–forming vegetables.

- Canned beans are a great shortcut, but to reduce flatulence, drain the liquid and rinse the beans before using them.
- Lentils are the fast-cooking legume. They need no presoaking and cook up quickly.

In addition, try these serving suggestions:

- Add legumes to soups, stews, and casseroles. Serve them chilled in salads or pureed in dips.
- Add a can of beans to a can of prepared soup for a hearty lunch.
- Toss three types of canned beans together with an olive oil–based salad dressing for a quick three bean salad.
- Add a few tablespoons of beans to your green salads.

Grains and Cereals

Complimenting the legumes are the grains (Table 12.2). Together they provide a major source of protein in addition to carbohydrates and fiber. Each whole grain has its own unique combination of vitamins, minerals, fibers, and phytochemicals. Whole grains and their brans and germs are excellent sources of the B vitamins, vitamin E, and protein, as well as the minerals calcium, iron, magnesium, phosphorus, potassium, selenium, and zinc. Both rice and wheat bran are excellent sources of the insoluble fiber necessary for colon health. Remember to always eat a vitamin C source with whole grains to increase mineral absorption. Foods made with wheat can be inflammatory, so limit the

Table 12.2 Sources of Whole Grains and Cereals

WHOLE GRAINS	WHOLE-GRAIN PRODUCTS
Amaranth	Pasta
Barley	Bread
Buckwheat	Crackers
Kamut	Flour
Millet	Air-popped popcorn
Oats	Cereals (hot and cold with no
Quinoa	added sugar)
Brown and wild rice	Bran (oat, rice, wheat)
Rye	Germ (wheat, rice polish)
Spelt	
Triticale	
Wheat	

amount of wheat-based cereals, pasta, breads, and other baked goods you eat. Explore the other grains too.

Each of the following servings contains approximately 15 grams of carbohydrates:

- 1 slice whole-grain bread
- ½ bun, bagel, or English muffin
- ¾ cup dry ready-to-eat cereal
- ½ cup cooked cereal, rice, corn, pasta, or root vegetables (such as yams, potatoes, or rutabagas)
- ⅓ cup cooked beans, peas, or lentils, or bean spread
- 3 cups popcorn

Here are some grain preparation tips:

- Rinse raw grain in cold water if it looks dirty or you see foreign particles. If you have purchased your grain from a bin, it is a good idea to rinse it well.

- Rinsing grain removes excess starch that clings to the surface and can make grains sticky instead of fluffy.
- To dry roast grains before cooking, put amaranth, rice, bulgur (cracked wheat), or buckwheat in a dry frying pan, place over medium heat, and stir until grains deepen in color. Cook as usual.

In addition, try these serving suggestions:

- Whole-grain pastas and hot cereals such as nine-grain or steel-cut oats are easy ways to put more grain variety into your diet. Serve the cereals with rice, soy, or almond milk. For hot savory meals, cook grain dishes like brown rice, teff, amaranth, millet, quinoa, spelt, or wild rice.
- Cold grain salads such as tabbouleh, Kamut, or bulgur can be soothing to a sore throat. Cook the grains in a vegetable or nonfat chicken broth to give them depth of flavor without the irritating seasonings that may be too strong after chemotherapy.
- Cook a week's worth of whole grains and store in the refrigerator. Add them to soups or casseroles.
- Grain products such as bulgur, semolina (wheat pasta pellets), and cornmeal can be cooked in the same way as whole grains. These products contain delicate oils, so they must be refrigerated in airtight containers to retain their nutrient value and to keep them from becoming rancid.
- Buy mixed whole-grain bread and bread with nuts and seeds. The sandwiches made from these breads

---

Foods to Avoid

Refined pastries and sweets

Deep-fried anything

Whole-milk and cream products, including sour cream

Soft drinks, sweetened and noncaloric

Artificial sweeteners

---

are more filling and interesting than those made from blah white bread.

- Have two or three boxes of dry cereal on hand in case you get bored with what you have. Don't buy the variety packs—they only include high-sugar, low-fiber cereals. Instead buy cereals that contain oats, barley, and bran.

Root Vegetables

Yams and sweet potatoes are not only excellent energy sources, they are also sources of antioxidant carotenes. Potatoes can have a high glycemic load, but they are also the highest food on the satiety index, a measure of how satisfying a food is and how long it takes before the eater is hungry again. Avoid high-starch potatoes such as Idaho, russet, and baking potatoes. Instead chose waxy potatoes such as new or baby potatoes, white round, Yukon gold, Finnish yellow, red, and fingerling potatoes.

Here are some preparation tips:

- Store potatoes and other root vegetables in a cool, dark area. Direct sunlight can turn potatoes green

and make them bitter. Cut or scrape off any green areas on potatoes before cooking.
- Don't store potatoes in the refrigerator; it causes the starch to turn to sugar, ruining the potato.

In addition, try these serving suggestions:

- Steam, bake, pressure-cook, or sauté potatoes and vegetables with 1 teaspoon olive oil. Stuff baked veggies with grains or beans.
- Season sweet potatoes and yams with nutmeg, cinnamon, allspice, and mace.

Vegetable Group

Red, yellow, and green vegetables are carotene-rich foods containing beta-carotene, other carotenoids, and vitamin C, which act as free radical scavengers, stimulate the immune system, and may even be toxic to tumors. Consistent epidemiological findings show a strong association between high beta-carotene intake and reduced incidence of squamous cell carcinomas, even in smokers. These veggies also contain cancer-fighting phytochemicals such as calcium, indoles, phthalides, ellagic acid, and flavonoids. Green leafy vegetables contain soluble and insoluble fiber, which increases stool bulk and dilutes possible harmful substances in the intestinal tract. A chemical called indole-3-carbinol—found in broccoli, cauliflower and cabbage—can increase the levels of BRCA1 and BRCA2 proteins (produced from the BRCA1 and BRCA2 genes), which repair damaged DNA.

Each of the following equals one vegetable serving in the diets in this book, and each contains 5 grams of carbohydrates. Only count a vegetable as a carbohydrate if you have three or more in one meal.

- 1 cup raw vegetables
- 1 cup canned tomatoes or tomato sauce
- 1 cup tomato/vegetable juice cocktail or clamato juice
- ½ cup cooked vegetable
- ½ cup chopped vegetable
- 1 medium vegetable
- ⅛ medium avocado
- 10 small or 5 large olives
- 2 tablespoons tomato sauce

You should eat at least one serving of cruciferous vegetables—broccoli, cauliflower, brussels sprouts, collard or mustard greens, the cabbage family—and two servings of green leafy vegetables (Table 12.3) a day.

Try these serving suggestions:

- Chop and add cruciferous vegetables to casseroles or salads.
- Sauté with tofu and seeds. Mix 1 cup olive oil, 1 cup balsamic vinegar, and 2 tablespoons sesame seeds; sprinkle over the top of raw chopped cabbage and cauliflower.
- Steam brussels sprouts and top with a shaving of butter.
- Dip cauliflower heads into ranch dressing for a light snack.
- Boil and mash cauliflower just as you would potatoes.

Table 12.3 Leafy Green Vegetables

Turnip greens	Radicchio
Collard greens	Beet tops
Mustard greens	Arugula (rocket)
Green and red romaine lettuce	Sliced and chopped cabbage
Green and red oak leaf lettuce	Tot soi
Green and red leaf lettuce	Green curly kale
Butterhead lettuce	Frisée
Spinach greens	Pea greens
Mizuna	Dandelion greens
Mâche	Cilantro
Ruby chard	Parsley
Belgian endive	Lemon balm
Sorrel	Fennel
	Dill

Here are some serving suggestions:

- The best way to cook nonstarchy vegetables is to steam them. If you do not have a steamer machine, put a metal steamer basket inside a large saucepan. Add water, being careful to keep the top from touching the basket. Lay the food to be steamed in the basket and cover with a tight lid. Make sure the water does not go dry.
- Green leafy vegetables cook quickly; steam or sauté them for just one or two minutes. Serve with tofu or bean dishes.
- Buy organic bagged salad mixes for easy, quick salads.
- Steam or sauté vegetables with 1 tablespoon extra-virgin olive oil and 1 teaspoon sesame seeds.
- Serve greens with a splash of tamari or soy sauce.

Antioxidant Vegetables

Eat at least two servings of antioxidant vegetables (Table 12.4) per day. Men should eat at least one serving of tomatoes per day for the lycopene. Onions are a rich source of quercetin, an antioxidant flavonoid. Bell peppers are rich sources of vitamin C, and garlic contains a large number of protective sulfur compounds.

Sea Vegetables

Sea vegetables—such as kelp, kombu, wakame, agar, dulse, carrageenan (Irish moss), nori, or sea lettuce—contain thyroid-stimulating substances and are loaded with the minerals calcium, potassium, iron, phosphorus, and iodine. They are high in fiber, low in fat, and contain vitamins A and B complex, as well as small quantities of vitamin C. Other important vegetables that you should eat are included in Table 12.5. Try these serving suggestions:

- Steam, stir-fry, sauté, or layer veggies in a casserole.
- Add raw vegetables to sandwiches.
- Sea vegetables can be crushed or chopped and added to soups, stews, stir-fry, or salads.

Table 12.4 Antioxidant Vegetables

Asparagus	Green peas
Bell peppers	Hot peppers
Carrots	Leeks
Corn	Onions
Garlic	Okra
Green beans	Pumpkin
Tomatoes	

Table 12.5 Other Vegetables

Shiitake, maitake, reishi, or mushroom extract	Celery
	Cucumbers
Turnips	Radishes
Rutabagas	Snow peas
Beets	Water chestnuts
Winter and summer squash	Zucchini
Artichokes	Bamboo shoots

Fruit Group

Fruits provide carbohydrates, vitamins, minerals, antioxidants, and other nutrients. They contain almost no protein or fat. Eat at least two servings of fruit (Table 12.6) per day including one serving of citrus, and at least two servings of berries per week.

Some types of fruit—especially apples, pears, and citrus fruits—are rich in soluble fiber. The flavonoids in berries contain some of the most powerful antioxidants. Orange and red fruits—including apricots, cantaloupe,

Table 12.6 Types of Fruit

Citrus fruit (oranges, lemons, grapefruit, tangerines)
Berries (blueberries, blackberries, strawberries, raspberries, marionberries, pomegranates)
Melons (watermelon, cantaloupe, honeydew)
Tropical fruit (pineapple, mango, papaya)
Dried fruit (figs, dates, raisins, prunes)
Stewed fruit (applesauce)
Other fresh fruits (bananas, cherries, plums, peaches, apricots, apples, pears)

mangoes, papayas, peaches, and watermelon—are good sources of the carotenes. Pomegranates have the highest level of antioxidants of any fruit. Dried plums (prunes) have triple the antioxidant ability of blueberries. So if you're sick of that morning bowl of bran, just three dried plums will give you the same amount of fiber. Dried fruits offer concentrated amounts of vitamins, minerals, and fiber while satisfying your sweet tooth. Drink water with these foods to help digestion. Avoid those treated with sulfur or other preservatives.

Swedish researchers found that eating bananas, carrots, and beets may lower the risk of developing kidney cancer. Women who ate bananas four to six times a week were 50 percent less likely to develop kidney cancer than those who did not eat them. Those who ate root veggies such as carrots and beets were 50 to 65 percent less likely to develop kidney cancer.

Each of the following servings of fruit contains approximately 15 grams of carbohydrates. For packaged fruit, check the label.

- ½ large fruit (pear, grapefruit, papaya, mango, pomegranate, or banana)
- 1 small to medium fruit (apple, peach, nectarine, orange, or kiwi)
- ½ cup (4 ounces) applesauce or juice-packed fruit
- 1 cup raw fruit
- ¾ cup berries
- ½ cup (4 ounces) fruit juice
- ¼ cup (2 ounces) dried fruit
- 2 canned peach halves
- ⅛ melon

Each of the following half-servings contains approximately 7.5 grams of carbohydrates:

- 2 apricots or dried prunes
- 1 small tangerine
- ¾ cup strawberries or watermelon cubes

Try these suggestions for serving fruit:

- Remove the skin, if the fruit is not organic, to reduce any pesticide residue.
- Fruits can be served raw, steamed, or baked.
- Baked apples with a sprinkle of cinnamon and a drizzle of honey are easy to digest, and the aroma of baking fruit is an appetite stimulant.
- Poach pears in wine and serve with a drizzle of dark chocolate sauce for an appealing dessert.
- Dilute one part juice with one part water for a less concentrated drink.

Protein Group

The protein group includes milk and dairy foods, eggs, noncarbohydrate soy foods, red meat, poultry, fish, and nuts and seeds. This group supplies protein, a nutrient necessary for the repair and maintenance of tissues. Protein is found in almost all foods (like the legumes mentioned earlier), but the richest source is muscle from red meat, poultry, and fish. Although we tend to think of animal protein as superior to plant protein, this is not true. Animal protein comes packaged with lots of fat, few vitamins and minerals, and no fiber, whereas plant protein is accompanied by lots of vitamins, minerals, and fiber. In addition, animal fat, like saturated fat, is a major source of **arachidonic acid**—a fatty acid that promotes inflammation.

To prevent inflammation and the effects it can have on cancer cells, you should get most of your protein from plant sources. (Take a look at Table 12.7 to get a list of inflammatory and anti-inflammatory foods). Legumes and grains are good protein sources. Fish (with an emphasis on fatty fish) and small amounts of lean poultry meat can also be part of your diet. Fatty fish contains EPA and DHA, two fatty acids that counter the effects of arachidonic acid and reduce inflammation. This includes mackerel (canned and fresh), herring, sardines, skipjack tuna, lake trout, and salmon (wild has more EPA and DHA).

Meat, eggs, milk, and poultry from organically fed animals are available via mail-order if you do not have a local supplier. Unlike the products in your supermarket, naturally fed animals produce foods with higher levels of omega-3 fats and no antibiotics, hormones, or other additives, so they can be part of your diet. Because they are grass fed, they also contain conjugated linolenic acid, a fat with anticancer properties of its own.

Do not eat shark, swordfish, king mackerel, tilefish, or canned tuna (due to concerns about methylmercury contamination). When you are recovered, you can add small amounts of these fish back into your diet. Avoid deep-fried foods and poultry with skin.

The protein foods in the following list do not contain carbohydrates. If you count carbs, they are free foods. If

Table 12.7 Inflammatory and Anti-Inflammatory Foods

INFLAMMATORY FOODS

Safflower, sunflower, corn, sesame, grapeseed, and soy oil

Peanut oil and dressings made with it

Margarines made with the preceding oils

Vegetable shortening, hydrogenated fats

Beef, pork, and organ meat

Ham, lunch meats, bacon

Full-fat milk, yogurt, and cottage cheese

Ice cream

Wheat products (pasta, bread)

Egg yolks

Refined and processed foods

ANTI-INFLAMMATORY FOODS

Flaxseed and flax oil

Fish oil

Olives, olive oil, and dressings made with it

Canola oil and dressings/margarines made with it

Mackerel (canned), herring, sardines, anchovies, wild
   salmon

Skipjack tuna (fresh, not canned)

Apples

Onions, leeks, and garlic

Berries (blueberries, raspberries, and strawberries)

Grape juice (purple)

Pumpkin seeds

Walnuts

you count calories or fat, they are not. You should eat two servings per day. One protein exchange (serving of protein) equals 3 ounces—about the size of a deck of cards.

- 3 to 4 ounces of low-fat red meat (once or twice a month)
- 3 to 4 ounces of fish, calamari, or shellfish, including lobster, shrimp, clams
- 3 ounces of tofu
- 3 ounces of nut butter
- 1 egg or 1 egg white (3 egg yolks per week) from hens fed with organic vegetarian feed
- 2 tablespoons of peanut butter (natural style)
- 1½ ounces of cheese
- ½ cup cottage cheese

Dairy Foods

Dairy foods (except cheese) also contain milk sugar, or lactose, so they must be included if you count carbohydrates. Drink only nonfat or 1 percent milk or instant powdered or dry nonfat milk. Buttermilk, acidophilus milk, and yogurt are cultured with beneficial bacteria.

Each of the following servings of milk contains 15 grams of carbohydrates:

- 1 cup of 1 percent or skim milk or plain nonfat yogurt
- ¾ cup flavored nonfat yogurt (low-carb)
- ½ cup evaporated milk
- ⅓ cup nonfat dry milk

Try these serving suggestions:

- Top bean and rice dishes with a dollop of plain yogurt.

I Won't Give up My Meat and Eggs!

One of the hardest parts of this cancer diet is giving up red meat and eggs. There is a way around this. The fatty acid composition of the animal reflects the fatty acid composition of the diet it was fed. Unfortunately our food animals have diets that are just as bad as our own, if not worse. It is not meat that is bad for you—it's the meat's diet. Animals that are grass fed produce meat that is actually a good source of the omega-3 fats and lower in saturated fat.

The same goes for hens and the eggs they lay. You can even buy high-omega-3 eggs in the supermarket. However, only a tiny fraction of the beef produced in the United States is from grass-fed animals, so this treat comes at a price. Maureen buys hers from a local farmer, but you can order yours online (see Appendix A).

- Use yogurt as a base for shakes and smoothies.
- Use yogurt in place of sour cream or mayonnaise in dips and dressings.

Yogurt is milk treated with healthy strains of bacteria such as *Lactobacillus bulgaricus*, *Lactobacillus acidophilus*, and *Streptococcus thermophilus*. It provides protein, calcium, and other vitamins and minerals. The bacteria in yogurt promote the regrowth of the healthy microflora in the gut after they have been killed by antibiotics, chemotherapeutic agents, or radiation. A healthy balance of intestinal bacteria is important for the proper digestion of fiber and absorption of vitamins. Yogurt that contains live cultures will have this fact marked on the label; look for it.

Soy Foods

Soy appears to have many benefits in the treatment of cancer. Eating one serving of soy (Table 12.8) every day may decrease the risk of developing a number of cancers by nearly 40 percent. Soy also has a cholesterol-lowering effect. Soybeans contain **phytoesterols**, which help protect against heart disease and are effective against skin cancer. Soy contains **saponins**, which are antioxidants and play a role in cancer prevention.

Genistein, an isoflavone found in soy products, is protective against leukemia and cancer of the colon, breast, lung, prostate, and skin. Oncogenes produce enzymes that can cause our cells to mutate dangerously and become cancer cells. One of those dangerous enzymes produced by the oncogenes is tyrosine protein kinase, a cell growth stimulator. Genistein is a potent inhibitor of tyrosine protein kinase, and it also appears to be an effective anticarcinogen against other enzymes involved in the cancer process. Soy also contains protease inhibitors, which appear to inhibit or prevent cancer growth.

Soy's role in hormone-related cancers has not yet been clarified, so do not take a concentrated soy supplement or isoflavone extract unless you are under the care of a knowledgeable physician. Instead of supplementing your diet with soy protein, use whey protein in your smoothies. It offers benefits too.

Table 12.8 Soy Foods

Soy milk (regular, low-fat, nonfat, fortified, vanilla, chocolate, carob)	Soy nuts
	Soy flour
	Soy grits
Tofu	Soy cheese
Tempeh	Miso

Try these serving suggestions:

- Organic soy milk is an easy, delicious way to put soy foods into your diet. Use soy milk on cereals, in hot drinks, and in cooking.
- Make soy milk smoothies or scrambled tofu instead of eggs. (Sauté half a chopped onion in 1 tablespoon of extra-virgin olive oil. Add 16 ounces crumbled firm tofu and sauté until heated through. Sprinkle with turmeric powder and soy sauce and serve.)
- Make soy cheese sandwiches, crumble tofu to replace tuna or egg in a tuna or egg salad sandwich, snack on soy nuts, and add cubes of miso to soups.
- For a healthful dip, combine 16 ounces tofu and 1 avocado in the blender.
- Use tofu in place of hamburger in tacos; add the taco seasoning directly to sautéed tofu.
- Blend silken tofu instead of evaporated milk into creamed soups, cream sauces, and puddings or pie fillings.
- Marinate strips of tofu with tamari, honey, sesame seeds, and fresh ginger to eat cold as snacks.
- Slice tempeh and brush the top with barbecue sauce for a grilled meal.
- Miso can be used for flavoring or to make soups.

Nuts, Seeds, and Seasonings

Nuts and seeds are excellent sources of protein and fiber. They are also high in heart-healthy fats and contain no cholesterol. They belong to both the protein group and the fats and oil group. For those wishing to gain weight, nuts and seeds and their butters are a high-calorie protein source. You should have at least one serving a day and can enjoy them raw or roasted and unsalted:

- Fresh nuts (almonds, Brazil nuts, cashews, filberts, pecans, pine nuts, pistachios, and walnuts)
- Fresh unseasoned seeds (pumpkin seeds, sesame seeds, sunflower seeds, flaxseed)
- Roasted unsalted peanuts (technically a legume)
- Nut and seed butters (tahini or sesame seed butter, walnut butter, almond butter, hazelnut butter, cashew butter, sunflower butter, and peanut butter)
- Nut milks

Peanuts are technically legumes but are usually classi-fied as nuts because of the similarities. Peanuts contain resveratrol, and roasting them increases the amount of an antioxidant flavonoid called p-coumaric acid. A small handful of almonds or walnuts makes a hearty-healthy snack that contains oils to prevent inflammation.

Try these serving suggestions:

- Nuts can be eaten whole as snacks, added to salads, or cooked with vegetables.
- Add nut butters to sauces and soups, or use as spreads in sandwiches or on crackers.
- Eat peanut butter on toast, in cookies, on celery, on crackers, or on a spoon.

We provide more serving suggestions for nuts and seeds in Chapter 16, as they can help when you are trying to gain weight.

In addition, use the seasonings in Table 12.9 liberally.

Fats and Oils

Most of the fats you eat will be hidden inside prepared or processed foods. High-fat foods and bakery goods include cakes, cookies, pies, muffins, donuts, and anything with cheese. Fats and oils do not contain carbohydrates or protein so they are not considered when counting carbs. Each of the following fat servings provides 5 grams of fat:

- 6 almonds or 10 small peanuts
- ⅛ avocado
- 1 teaspoon oil or margarine
- 6 small olives
- 2 tablespoons low-calorie salad dressing
- 1 tablespoon regular salad dressing
- 1 tablespoon cocoa (unsweetened)
- 1 teaspoon butter, oil, or margarine
- 2 teaspoons mayonnaise or nut butter
- 1 tablespoon salad dressing
- 1 tablespoon cream cheese
- 2 teaspoons low-fat margarine or spread

Several factors need to be considered when evaluating oils: their monounsaturated fatty acid content, their anti-

Table 12.9 Seasonings

Garlic, onions, leeks, and scallions (raw or cooked)	Cumin
	Basil
Gingerroot (juiced, raw, brewed)	Caraway seeds
Hot peppers (dried, raw, cooked)	Cloves
Rosemary	Tarragon
Curry	Turmeric

oxidant content, and their omega-6-to-omega-3 ratio. Oils contain a mixture of omega-3, omega-6, and omega-9 fatty acids. Oils that have a high level of monounsaturated fats have more omega-3 fatty acids and so do not promote inflammation. Oils that have a high level of polyunsaturated fatty acids have a higher level of omega-6 fatty acids and can promote inflammation if eaten in excess. Saturated fatty acids are associated with heart disease and also contain arachidonic acid which promotes inflammation. Most of the fats in your diet should be rich in monounsaturated fats.

Recommended fats and oils include the following:

- Oils that have a high level of monounsaturated fatty acids and more omega-3 than omega-6 fatty acids
- Cold-pressed canola oil and dressings and mayonnaise made with canola oil
- Extra-virgin olive oil and dressings made with olive oil
- Flaxseed oil and dressings made from it

Try these serving suggestions:

- Use your measuring spoons when you need a serving of fat. It is very easy to overestimate quantities.
- Choose oils that are cold pressed and minimally processed when you're making a dressing. Choose refined canola oil for cooking.
- A good oil will identify itself by its packaging. They are usually sold in small quantities to keep them fresh. Good oils should be stored in a dark, cool environment to reduce their exposure to light and oxygen. We store ours in the refrigerator. Flaxseed and other oils rich in the polyunsaturated

essential fatty acids are fragile and should be stored in dark bottles.

- Whenever you need to combine a sweet food with oil, choose cold-pressed canola oil because of its mild flavor.
- Extra-virgin olive oil makes excellent dressings and flavoring agents.
- If you must use a margarine, buy a soft tub brand, liquid margarine, or a spread, and use it sparingly. These types have a lower percentage of hydrogenated oils and fewer trans-fatty acids. However, they are also high in inflammatory omega-6 fatty acids. Mayonnaise is almost all fat, so use it sparingly too and buy a brand that contains only canola oil.
- Always check the label of prepared foods to identify those that are high in fat. Never make high-fat foods a habit. Save them for occasional treats.

Food Preparation

How you prepare your food is almost as important as how you choose your food. It does your body no good to take a piece of EPA/DHA–rich salmon and deep-fry it into nuggets of saturated fat. Likewise, boiling fresh organic vegetables in water until they are limp shadows of their former nutrient-rich selves makes no sense.

Here are a few helpful suggestions for preparing food:

- Buy some cookbooks aimed at healthful eating.
- Expand your definition of grains beyond wheat, and learn how to cook with soy.

• Give your kitchen a makeover. This makes a great weekend project. It can also be quite aerobic. Get rid of the high-salt, high-fat, and high-sugar foods. Load them into boxes and give them to the teenager down the street. Remember, if it's not in the house, you can't eat it.

• Restock your pantry with whole foods. Get acquainted with the health food section of your store and visit a few health food stores. Buy some whole-grain breakfast cereals, brown bread, and brown rice. You will be amazed at some of the great healthy snack foods available.

• Think about getting some new cookware, such as a juicer, pressure cooker, food steamer, or Crock-Pot.

Using a Juicer

Juicing is the victim of black-or-white reasoning. Supporters believe the "juice pushers" on the TV infomercials and consider fresh juices a cure for everything. Critics dismiss the whole idea as another silly fad. The truth, as always, lies somewhere in between.

Juice extractors work by splitting open the cell wall of the plant and separating the cytoplasm and other liquid components from the cell walls and other fibrous parts. The liquid portion, or juice, contains any vitamin and flavor components and some of the pectins that were in the cytoplasm. The solid portion, or pulp, contains the cellulose, lignin, and remaining pectins found in the cell walls. Since juices by definition lack fiber, they should never be used to replace the five fruits and vegetables a day your body needs.

Juices have been criticized because they lack fiber, but their therapeutic value lies in just this quality. The average person would have difficulty eating a pound of carrots, but this same amount juiced becomes a quickly consumed eight ounces. A juicer will allow you to increase your consumption of fruits and vegetables at a time when you may not feel like eating due to mouth sores, a sore throat, difficulty in chewing and swallowing, early satiety, lack of appetite, or just plain dislike of vegetables in general. It is the only way to get fruits and vegetables into you when you're on a low-fiber diet.

As handy as food supplements are, they cannot replace whole foods. Consider, for example, beta-carotene supplements. We are told that in large doses beta-carotene is nontoxic, and it is. The more beta-carotene consumed, the higher the blood levels of beta-carotene. But high beta-carotene levels are also associated with a decrease in blood levels of the other carotenes, some of which are more powerful antioxidants than beta-carotene. Recent studies indicate that beta-carotene may compete for absorption with the other carotenes.

Juice, unlike purified supplements, contains all of the carotenes present in the juiced food. So while juice is not a whole food, it is a wholesome food, and quite a few steps closer to whole than food supplements. Just be sure not to overdo it. We have talked to people who were drinking a gallon or two a day and to others who were consuming no foods, only juices. Please do not stress your body this way. Without adequate protein, your body will not be able to fight the cancer. One or two glasses of fresh vegetable juice are all you need.

Evaluate a juicer as you would any electrical appliance. The juice that is produced is the same, regardless of the type of machine. What differs between machines is the power of the motor and the ease of cleaning. We recommend a pulp ejector type, since they are the easiest to clean. Juice extractors can be found in any department store and some health food stores.

Using a Pressure Cooker

When you are tired or not feeling well from therapy, who wants to stand over a hot stove and cook? Pull up a chair and let a pressure cooker do the work for you. The advantages of today's safety-conscious pressure cookers are many:

- Pressure cookers prepare foods faster than any other cooking method, including the microwave. They make fast food healthy food. Whole grains such as brown rice cook in less than fifteen minutes.
- Food comes out moist, tender, and easy to swallow—important attributes when the mouth is dry or sore.
- The cooker seals in flavors and nutrients. Vegetables not only look great, but all of their flavors are retained, not lost to the air.
- Cooking odors are sealed in the pot. Food odor will not linger in the air for hours after, killing your appetite.
- By using the metal trivet in the cooker, you can cook foods in the serving dish, making cleanup a snap. This is a wonderful way to cook only one serving.

Skip the smaller models and buy one with a capacity of at least six quarts. This will enable you to pressure-steam foods in their serving dishes or let you cook a whole meal at once. Pressure cookers are currently enjoying a revival. They can be found in most department stores and discount houses.

Using a Food Steamer

Food steamers make grain and vegetable cooking simply goof proof. They are not as fast as pressure cookers, but they do not need to be watched. Just add the food and come back when the timer goes off. Steamers are particularly suited for delicate vegetables such as leafy greens. Small grains like quinoa or millet that can get gummy when cooked in a saucepan come out separate, fluffy, and much more appetizing in a steamer.

Food steamers come in many shapes and sizes. We suggest you buy a plastic food steamer rather than a metal rice cooker. The food steamers are much easier to clean and more versatile. Here's a summary of the benefits:

- You can't burn the pan with the steamer because it will automatically turn itself off when the water runs out.
- Steaming is one of the easiest ways to cook the whole grains necessary for colon health. Cook a week's worth of your favorite grain, and store it in the refrigerator. For a quick meal add a few table-spoons of the cooked grain to the steamer with some chopped leafy greens. Sprinkle with a marinade and reheat.
- Water-soluble flavors and vitamins are not lost to boiling water. Foods taste better and are better for you.

- Steamed foods are moist and tender. They do not hurt sore gum and mouth tissues and are easy to swallow when the throat is dry.
- Food steamers allow you to cook food in the serving bowl, making cleanup quick. Most plastic parts just require a simple wipe to clean.

As with the pressure cookers, larger is better. Buy one with a built-in timer so you will not have to remember when to turn it off. Food steamers are inexpensive and available everywhere.

Using a Crock-Pot

Slow cookers or Crock-Pots are making a comeback. They are the opposite of pressure cookers, cooking food slowly over a period of six to ten hours. You can use them to cook grains overnight or to cook bean and grain dishes while you are at work during the day. The benefits of slow cookers are similar to those of pressure cookers. Because foods cook at a very low temperature, fewer nutrients are boiled away. Like pressure cookers and steamers, the foods are flavorful and moist.

Now that you have an understanding of the food groups and ways to prepare them, we'll show you how to count your calories, carbohydrates, and fat intake.

13

Counting Calories, Carbs, and Fat: Making Your Diet Plan Work for You

Before you can start your diet you need to determine how many calories are appropriate for you. You should also use the chart in Table 13.1 to determine your body mass index. Your BMI can tell you if you need to lose weight. Calorie counting can become tedious at a time when your patience may already be strained by your health. To control the amount of sugar your tumor has access to from your blood, we strongly suggest you learn how to count carbohydrates. Once you know approximately how many calories you are eating now to maintain your present weight, you can look up how many carbohydrate grams you should eat each day and how many you should eat at each snack and meal. This technique is explained in the latter section of this chapter. It is used by many diabetics to determine their insulin dose, and it is easier to control your diet this way too.

Table 13.1 BMI (Body Mass Index) Table

	Normal		Moderately Overweight					Markedly Overweight					Obese					
BMI	**23**	**24**	**25**	**26**	**27**	**28**	**29**	**30**	**31**	**32**	**33**	**34**	**35**	**36**	**37**	**38**	**39**	**40**
Height (inches)								*Body Weight (pounds)*										
58	110	115	119	124	129	134	138	143	148	153	158	162	167	172	177	181	186	191
59	114	119	124	128	133	138	143	148	153	158	163	168	173	178	183	188	193	198
60	118	123	128	133	138	143	148	153	158	163	168	174	179	184	189	194	199	204
61	122	127	132	137	143	148	153	158	164	169	174	180	185	190	195	201	206	211
62	126	131	136	142	147	153	158	164	169	175	180	186	191	196	202	207	213	218
63	130	135	141	146	152	158	163	169	175	180	186	191	197	203	208	214	220	225
64	134	140	145	151	157	163	169	174	180	186	192	197	204	209	215	221	227	232
65	138	144	150	156	162	168	174	180	186	192	198	204	210	216	222	228	234	240
66	142	148	155	161	167	173	179	186	192	198	204	210	216	223	229	235	241	247
67	146	153	159	166	172	178	185	191	198	204	211	217	223	230	236	242	249	255
68	151	158	164	171	177	184	190	197	203	210	216	223	230	236	243	249	256	262
69	155	162	169	176	182	189	196	203	209	216	223	230	236	243	250	257	263	270
70	160	167	174	181	188	195	202	209	216	222	229	236	243	250	257	264	271	278
71	165	172	179	186	193	200	208	215	222	229	236	243	250	257	265	272	279	286
72	169	177	184	191	199	206	213	221	228	235	242	250	258	265	272	279	287	294
73	174	182	189	197	204	212	219	227	235	242	250	257	265	272	280	288	295	302
74	179	186	194	202	210	218	225	233	241	249	256	264	272	280	287	295	303	311
75	184	192	200	208	216	224	232	240	248	256	264	272	279	287	295	303	311	319
76	189	197	205	213	221	230	238	246	254	263	271	279	287	295	304	312	320	328

Source: National Heart, Lung, and Blood Institute (nhlbi.nih.gov/guidelines/obesity)

How to Calculate Your Caloric Intake

The two diets in Chapters 14 and 15 are explained in terms of charts based on your caloric intake. Unlike many diets, they are not based on an idealistic body weight (a number too low to be practical) but on your present weight. But before you can use these diets you must determine how many calories you use.

It takes our bodies a certain number of calories to maintain our weight. How many calories we burn is influenced by many factors, including gender, exercise level, genes, environment, health, and age. When we eat more calories than we burn, we gain weight, and when we eat less, we lose weight. Men burn more calories than women in part because men have a greater percentage of muscle tissue than women and muscle tissue burns more calories than fat. Also, we burn fewer calories as we age.

While we have little influence over our gender, genes, or health, we do have control over how many calories we eat and how much we exercise. It takes an excess of 3,500 calories to gain 1 pound. Therefore, to lose 1 pound, you must cut 3,500 calories. This is usually accomplished by cutting 500 calories a day, which results in a gentle weight loss of 1 pound a week. Now you can understand why it is impossible to lose the amount of weight that many diets and diet products advertise. You simply cannot lose 20 pounds in one week. You would have to cut 10,000 calories a day when you only eat 3,000. Your body can only burn fat so fast.

Basic Considerations for Calculating Caloric Intake

A bit of calculation is necessary to determine how many calories it takes for you to maintain your weight. This will be just a rough approximation. We use the following formulas because they are simple, but there are more accurate (and complex) formulas available on the Internet.

1. Choose the appropriate formula from the next few sections according to your exercise level and gender to calculate how many calories you eat each day

2. As we age, the number of calories we burn decreases.
   - If you are age thirty-one to fifty, subtract 200 calories.
   - If you are fifty-one or over, subtract 400 calories.
3. If you need to lose weight, subtract 500 calories from the total. This will give you a weight loss of approximately 1 to 2 pounds a week.
4. If you need to gain weight, add 500 calories to the total. But be careful not to gain weight too fast. Your goal is to gain both fat and lean muscle tissue, and that takes time. A weight gain of 4 pounds a month is a good goal.

Once you have determined your caloric intake, you can use the charts in each of the diets to determine the amount of fat, saturated fat, and carbohydrate grams and servings you should have.

If You Get Little Exercise

If you do very little exercise or have an inactive lifestyle, use this formula:

My weight: _____ pounds
Daily calorie requirement (men):
    Weight (in pounds) × 14 = _____ calories
Daily calorie requirement (women):
    Weight (in pounds) × 12 = _____ calories
If you are thirty-one to fifty, subtract 200 calories.
If you are fifty-one and over, subtract 400 calories.

Total number of calories to maintain your
   weight = _____
Do you need to lose weight? If yes, subtract
   500 calories = _____

Let's see how you would calculate your caloric intake if you are a thirty-year-old, 115 pound woman who gets no exercise. Your base level of calories is 115 × 12, which equals 1,380 calories a day. Since you don't need to lose weight and just want to maintain, you need to keep your caloric intake at 1,380 per day.

If You Get Moderate Exercise

If you live a moderately active lifestyle (with three or four exercise sessions per week), use this formula:

My weight: _____ pounds
Daily calorie requirement (men):
   Weight (in pounds) × 16 = _____ calories
Daily calorie requirement (women):
   Weight (in pounds) × 14 = _____ calories
If you are thirty-one to fifty, subtract 200 calories.
If you are fifty-one and over, subtract 400 calories.
Total number of calories to maintain your
   weight = _____
Do you need to lose weight? If yes, subtract
   500 calories = _____

Let's see how you would calculate how many calories it takes to maintain your present weight if you are a forty-five-year-old, 220-pound man who gets a moderate amount of exercise. Your base level of calories is 220 × 16, or 3,520 calories a day. Since you are over thirty, you must subtract 200 calories to give 3,320 calories. To lose weight you must subtract an additional 500 calories, so to calculate your total caloric intake, you would have

$$3,520 - 200 - 500 = 2,820 \text{ calories}$$

If You Have an Active Lifestyle

If you are very active and get five or more exercise sessions a week, use this formula:

My weight: _____ pounds
Daily calorie requirement (men):
    Weight (in pounds) × 18 = _____ calories
Daily calorie requirement (women):
    Weight (in pounds) × 16 = _____ calories
If you are thirty-one to fifty, subtract 200 calories.
If you are fifty-one and over, subtract 400 calories.
Total number of calories to maintain your
    weight = _____
Do you need to lose weight? If yes, subtract
    500 calories = _____

If a whole-foods diet is going to be a big change for you, don't decrease calories for the first month. Wait and see how your body reacts to your new food choices. Many people will lose weight without decreasing calories because of the volume of food and increase in fiber.

The Mifflin–St. Jeor Equation

A more accurate way to calculate your caloric intake is to use the Mifflin–St. Jeor equation, often used by health professionals.

Women: [10 × weight (kg)] + [6.25 × height (cm)] − [5 × age (years)] − 161 = _____

Men: [10 × weight (kg)] + [6.25 × height (cm)] − [5 × age (years)] + 5 = _____

Finally you must make an adjustment for your activity level; multiply the number by one of the following:

  1.3 for sedentary individuals (e.g., office workers)
  1.4 for moderately active adults
  1.5 for very active adults

Carbohydrate Counting

Carbohydrates are the macronutrients that directly affect your blood sugar level, so when you want to control your blood sugar, it makes sense to control your dietary carbohydrates. Fifty-five percent of your daily calories should come from carbs, but most people haven't a clue what "55 percent of calories" means or how to translate that percentage into food. Carbohydrate counting is a useful technique that helps you to structure your diet without having to count calories. It is popular among people with diabetes who use it to calculate how much insulin to inject. Carb counting can help you achieve a balanced diet that avoids spikes in blood sugar.

There are five steps to counting carbs:

1. Understand the definition of *carbohydrate*.
2. Understand the meaning of *carbohydrate servings*.
3. Determine how many carbohydrate servings you are allotted each day.
4. Determine how many carbohydrate servings you should eat at each meal or snack.
5. Familiarize yourself with serving sizes of carb-containing foods.

What Is a Carbohydrate?

To understand what a carb is we strongly suggest you read Chapter 5, if you haven't already done so. A carbohydrate is one of the macronutrients (protein and fat are the other two). They are called macronutrients because they are the nutrients needed in the largest amounts. Carbohydrates provide immediate energy for the body.

There are three types of carbohydrates: sugars, starches, and fiber—the first two produce energy and are broken down into glucose. No matter what the source of the carbohydrate, it is broken down into the same unit—the glucose molecule. When the pancreas senses glucose, it releases the hormone insulin which then unlocks the cells in the liver, fatty tissue, and muscles so glucose molecules can enter and feed the cell. Eating carbohydrate-rich foods that are quickly digested results in a sharp rise in blood glucose. Insulin secreted by your pancreas will decrease blood sugar, but not before your tumor can eat its fill too.

If you are overweight, chances are you are also insulin resistant. This means your cells resist the action of insulin so that glucose levels rise in the blood and remain that way longer. The following foods contain carbohydrates:

- Fruits, as well as fruit juices and products flavored with them
- Sugar, including sweeteners like honey and molasses and foods with sugar
- Milk and products made with milk such as yogurt, ice cream, and sour cream
- Starches such as grains, pasta, cereals, and baked goods
- Starchy vegetables such as potatoes and yams

What Is a Carbohydrate Serving?

When you count carbohydrates, you don't need to count every gram you eat, although some people do. Instead you count *servings* (or exchanges) of carbohydrates. Each serving contains roughly 15 grams of carbohydrates, so when you know how many servings you eat, you also know how many grams you eat. For now you can forget about protein and fat foods; they have no effect on your blood sugar levels.

Carbohydrate counting assumes that all carbohydrates are equal and have an equal effect on blood sugar levels. This is not necessarily true, of course. Your body has its differences, and so do the foods you eat. Carbohydrate-rich foods that have a low-glycemic index/load and whole foods that are rich in soluble fiber have less effect on glucose levels.

Each starch, fruit, and milk serving listed in Table 13.2 contains roughly 15 grams of carbohydrates. Proteins, fats, and most vegetables are not counted because they do not contain carbohydrates.

Use the chart in Table 13.3 for converting carbohydrates into servings. When you eat a packaged food, you must check the label for serving size and number of carbohydrates per serving. Be careful, because the serving sizes of packaged foods may not be the same as those in our chart. For example, if the label on a small snack-sized bag of chips says 15 carbohydrates, don't assume the whole bag, small as it is, is one serving. It may be two servings and the whole bag is then 30 grams. Very small serving sizes is one way some manufacturers make it look like a food has fewer calories than it really does. You should also use Table 13.3 for counting the carbs in a recipe when the grams of carbohydrate are given but you are confused about the serving size. All you need to know about a food is how many grams of carbohydrates it contains, then look it up on this chart.

How Do I Know How Many Carbohydrates I'm Allotted?

It's easy. All you need to know is your present caloric intake, which you calculated earlier in this chapter. Your carbohydrate and fat grams and servings are listed by calorie level. The number of carbohydrates you are allotted is determined by two factors: what percentage of your diet is made up of carbohydrates and how many calories you eat.

Table 13.2 Individual Serving Sizes of Carbohydrates
(15 grams)

FOOD GROUP	AMOUNT PER SERVING
Starches	1 slice bread
	⅓ cup cooked pasta, cooked grains, hot cereals, and legumes
	¾ cup dry cereal
	3 cups popcorn
	4–6 crackers
Starchy vegetables	½ cup peas, corn, yams, sweet potatoes, or potatoes
	¾ cup winter squash or canned pumpkin
Fruit	1 small piece fruit
	½ cup fruit juice
Milk	1 cup milk
	¾ cup plain yogurt
Desserts	2 small cookies
	½ cup ice cream
Packaged foods	½ cup of any casserole, like tuna or chicken noodle, macaroni and cheese, chili with meat, or spaghetti and meat sauce
	1 cup cream, bean, tomato, or vegetable soup
	1 cup beef and vegetable stew
	⅛ of a 10-inch pizza
	½ store-bought pot pie, such as chicken, turkey, or beef
	One 3-ounce taco

Table 13.3 Converting Carbs into Servings

CARB GRAMS	SERVINGS
0–5	Do not count
6–10	½ serving
11–20	1 serving
21–25	1½ servings
26–35	2 servings

Chapters 14 and 15 contain two diets: one is 55/15/30 and the other is 45/25/30. When a diet is expressed this way, the first number is the percentage of carbohydrates, the second is the protein percentage, and the last is the fat percentage. (It is sometimes called the **CPF ratio**.) One hundred percent of calories means the total of all the calories you are to eat for the day.

You cannot eat more than the sum of your total calories. Therefore, the amount of calories of the three macronutrients must always equal 100 percent. When you take any percentage away from one nutrient, you must put it in one of the other two. If you wanted more than 55 percent of carbohydrates in your diet, you would have to subtract the excess from either protein or fat. A diet with 65 percent of calories from carbs would have to subtract the extra 10 percent from protein or fat, or we can split the difference and take 5 percent from each so now our diet is 65/10/25. As you can see, this is a low–fat diet. We've seen clients who want to have a high-carb, high-protein, high-fat diet such as 65/30/40, but it is impossible to eat more than 100 percent of your calories. Likewise you cannot eat less than 100 percent.

Table 13.4 Fat Grams and Servings by Caloric Intake (taken from Table 14.1)

CALORIES	FAT CALORIES	FAT GRAMS	FAT SERVINGS	SAT. FAT CAL	SAT. FAT GRAMS
2,000	600	67	13	140	16

Let's say you prefer a high-carb, low-fat diet, so your percentage of carbohydrates is 55 percent. Now you must determine 55 percent of what. The charts for the following calculations are found in Chapter 14, but excerpts from these charts are included here for your convenience. Let's say your calculations find that you eat 2,000 calories. Look at the chart in Table 13.4; the number of calories is in the first column, and you can run your finger across to see how many grams and servings of fat you should eat. You can eat 600 calories from fat, which is 67 grams of fat and 13 fat servings. You should also eat no more than 16 grams of saturated fat.

Now look at the chart in Table 13.5. It tells you to eat 275 grams of carbohydrates, which is 18 servings.

Not all people have the same metabolism, so the number of calories you need to maintain your weight may not be the same for someone else. We all know at least one person who can eat piles of food and never gain weight. We also know those who look at a carb and put on pounds.

Table 13.5 Carb Grams and Servings by Caloric Intake (taken from Table 14.2)

CALORIES	CARB CALORIES	CARB GRAMS	CARB SERVINGS
2,000	1,100	275	18

Table 13.6 Carbohydrate Distribution by Caloric Intake
(taken from Table 14.3)

CALORIES	BREAKFAST	SNACK	LUNCH	SNACK	DINNER	SNACK	TOTAL
2,000	4	1	5	1	5	2	18

Determine How Many Carb Servings You Should Eat at Each Meal or Snack

In order to keep your blood glucose levels even, it is best if you eat frequently throughout the day. Look at the chart in Table 13.6. Again, your calorie level is in the first column; the rest of the columns explain how to distribute your carbohydrate servings.

This plan calls for three meals and three snacks. Your work schedule will probably determine when you eat your three large meals; distribute the snacks so you don't go more than four hours without eating. Your longest fast should be overnight. It is important you eat your nighttime snack; these are the carbohydrates that will keep your body fueled during the night.

This meal plan is just a suggestion. For example, you may need a smaller snack in the morning but a larger one in the afternoon. The longer the period between meals, the larger the next meal or snack should be.

Fat Counting

The tables in Chapters 14 and 15 show how many servings a day are appropriate for your calorie level. This amount includes the fats used in cooking and seasoning and those found in other foods such as meat. In general,

- 1 tablespoon of a fat or oil = 120 calories
- 2 tablespoons of dressing = 150 calories

Carbohydrate counting will help you control your carbohydrate intake. After you have been on one of our diets for a month and have seen your body's response to the new food, you can determine if you also need to keep track of how many calories you eat. This won't be neces sary for many of you because the foods that you eat in excess are not found in these diets. You will be losing 4 to 6 pounds a month just by eliminating the white flour and refined foods.

If weight control does become necessary, you will need to cut back on your fat intake or learn how to count fats. Counting fats is a lot easier and less restrictive than counting calories. You will find the appropriate amount of fat for your caloric intake in your diet prescription. These grams do not have to be as evenly distributed as your carbohydrate grams. What counts is the total amount.

Most people find they need to eat fat with carbs or protein with carbs. You do not have to have servings of all three nutrients at each meal no matter who claims you must. There is nothing magical about eating the same macronutrient percentages at each meal.

14

Higher Carb, Lower Fat Diet

This diet can be described as higher carbohydrate and lower fat. As a whole-foods diet, the meals have a naturally low glycemic load that can deprive a tumor of nourishment. It is rich in antioxidants, fiber, and the monounsaturated fats that can protect your tissues from oxidative stress. It's low in saturated fats and the arachidonic acid that can cause inflammation but high in the omega-3 fatty acids that can prevent inflammation.

Is this diet right for you, or should you try the one in the next chapter? Let your body make the choice. If you want to lose weight, both diets will be successful, it is just a matter of which one will cause you the least hunger. This diet avoids the refined and processed foods that stimulate carbohydrate cravings in some people while still providing your body and brain with the carbohydrates it needs. So give this diet a try first even if you have had problems sticking to a high-carb diet before. If after six months you have a problem with appetite or glucose control, then switch to the lower-carb diet.

If too much weight loss is a problem, follow the suggestions in the weight gain section in Chapter 16 and add those foods to this diet.

Calculating Your Higher Carb, Lower Fat Diet (55/15/30)

First take a look at the following macronutrient guidelines:

- 55 percent carbohydrates (stressing whole, unprocessed foods) from whole grains, legumes, and vegetables
- 15 percent protein (stressing legumes, nuts, and seeds) from beans, peas, and lentils
- 30 percent fat (10 percent from monounsaturated fat and 7 percent or less from saturated fat) from fish, poultry, flaxseed, fish oil, and olive oil
- Less than 300 milligrams of cholesterol

Next, look at the charts on fat grams and servings by caloric intake (Table 14.1) and carbohydrate grams and servings for each calorie level (Table 14.2). If your caloric intake is between calorie levels, move up or down toward the number that's closest to yours.

Once you have determined your caloric intake, use Table 14.3 to find the appropriate distribution of carbohydrates. This plan is based on three meals and three snacks.

Table 14.1 Fat Grams and Servings by Caloric Intake

CALORIES	FAT CALORIES	FAT GRAMS	FAT SERVINGS	SAT. FAT CAL	SAT. FAT GRAMS
1,400	420	47	9	98	11
1,600	480	53	11	112	12
1,800	540	60	12	126	14
2,000	600	67	13	140	16
2,200	660	73	15	154	17
2,400	720	80	16	168	19
2,600	780	87	17	182	20
2,800	840	93	19	196	22
3,000	900	100	20	210	23
3,200	960	107	21	224	25
3,400	1,020	113	23	238	26
3,600	1,080	120	24	252	28
3,800	1,140	127	25	266	30
4,000	1,200	133	27	280	31
4,200	1,260	140	28	294	33
4,400	1,320	147	30	308	34

Table 14.2 Carb Grams and Servings by Caloric Intake

CALORIES	CARB CALORIES	CARB GRAMS	CARB SERVINGS
1,400	770	193	13
1,600	880	220	15
1,800	990	248	17
2,000	1,100	275	18
2,200	1,210	303	20
2,400	1,320	330	22
2,600	1,430	358	24
2,800	1,540	385	26
3,000	1,650	413	28
3,200	1,760	440	29
3,400	1,870	468	31
3,600	1,980	495	33
3,800	2,090	523	35
4,000	2,200	550	37
4,200	2,310	578	39
4,400	2,420	605	40

Table 14.3 Carbohydrate Distribution by Caloric Intake (55/15/30)

CALORIES	BREAKFAST	SNACK	LUNCH	SNACK	DINNER	SNACK	TOTAL
1,400	3	1	3	1	4	1	13
1,600	3	1	4	1	5	1	15
1,800	4	1	4	1	5	2	17
2,000	4	1	5	1	5	2	18
2,200	4	2	5	2	5	2	20
2,400	5	2	5	2	6	2	22
2,600	5	2	6	2	7	2	24
2,800	6	2	6	2	7	3	26
3,000	6	2	7	2	8	3	28
3,200	7	2	7	2	8	3	29
3,400	7	2	8	2	9	3	31
3,600	8	3	8	2	9	3	33
3,800	8	3	8	3	10	3	35
4,000	9	3	9	3	10	3	37
4,200	9	3	9	3	11	4	39
4,400	9	3	10	3	11	4	40

Higher Carb, Lower Fat Meal Plans

The following meal plans are examples of the food choices you can make on this diet. We have included menus for 1,600, 1,800, and 2,000 calories (recipes for the entries marked with an star can be found in Chapter 18). Your caloric and carb intake will vary from day to day because it is impossible to eat any percentage of calories precisely. Here are a few helpful general guidelines to follow with any of these meal plans:

- Eat five to six small meals a day rather than two to three large ones.

- If you cannot manage to eat all of the recommended vegetable servings, try juicing some of them.
- Foods that taste sweet should be eaten only on a full stomach.
- Cook meals that are appealing to the eye as well as the palate.
- Drink eight to ten glasses of water (preferably filtered) a day.
- Whenever you are hungry, snack on high-protein foods. A handful of nuts is a good choice.
- Don't drink fluids or soups before or with meals. They will fill you up and leave no room for foods that are nutrient dense.
- Make mealtimes a pleasant experience by relaxing before a meal, eating with friends or family, and creating a pleasant atmosphere at the table.
- If you lose weight, increase serving sizes. If you gain weight, decrease serving sizes.

Meal Plan for 1,600 Calories

Total calories: 1,670
CPF ratio: 53/22/25

Breakfast
Banana-berry breakfast smoothie★   1 serving

Morning Snack
Vegetable juice   12 ounces
Walnuts   14 halves

Lunch

Green leaf lettuce	2 cups
Baked beans, vegetarian	1 cup
Olive oil and vinegar salad dressing	1 tablespoon
Tomato	4 wedges (1 medium tomato)

Afternoon Snack

Apple	1 medium

Dinner

Baked chicken breast, skin removed	3 ounces
Yams, baked	⅔ cup
Broccoli, chopped	1 cup
Lemon juice, fresh	1 teaspoon
Romaine lettuce, shredded	1½ cups
Olive oil dressing	1 tablespoon
Banana	1 medium
Coffee with 1 percent milk	1 cup

Evening Snack

Fruit cup in extra-light syrup	4 ounces

Basic Nutritional Summary

Calories: 1,670.16; protein: 92.37 grams; carbs: 225.08 grams; fat: 48.03 grams; saturated fat: 9.60 grams; cholesterol: 139.06 milligrams; sodium: 2,425.82 milligrams; fiber: 40.37 grams

Meal Plan for 1,800 Calories

Total calories: 1,771
CPF ratio: 55/19/26

Breakfast

Whole-grain bread	2 slices
Better butter with canola oil★	2 teaspoons
Blueberries	½ cup
Strawberries, sliced	½ cup

Morning Snack

Banana	1 medium

Lunch

Sourdough pita pocket	1 pita
Mackerel salad★	1 cup
Green leaf lettuce, shredded	1 cup
Baked beans, vegetarian	⅔ cup

Afternoon Snack

Apple	1 medium

Dinner

Coho salmon, wild	3 ounces
Yams, baked without salt	⅔ cup
Broccoli, chopped	1 cup
Olive oil	1 teaspoon
Lemon juice	1 teaspoon
Almonds, sliced	1 teaspoon
Romaine lettuce	2 cups

Olive oil dressing	1 tablespoon
Raisins	¼ cup
Blue cheese, crumbled	¼ cup

Evening Snack

| Tangerines | 2 small |

Basic Nutritional Summary

Calories: 1,770.77; protein: 84.38 grams; carbs: 249.07 grams; fat: 53.42 grams; saturated fat: 14.24 grams; cholesterol: 173.18 milligrams; sodium: 2,438.76 milligrams; fiber: 40.50 grams

Meal Plan for 2,000 Calories

Total Calories: 2,042
CPF ratio: 54/19/27

Breakfast

Flax Plus cereal	1½ cups
Milk, 1 percent or skim	6 ounces
Strawberries, sliced	1 cup

Morning Snack

| Walnuts | 1 ounce or 14 halves |
| Grapes | 1 cup |

Lunch

| Peanut butter and jelly sandwich | 1 serving |
| Milk, 1 percent or skim | 8 ounces |

Afternoon Snack

Vegetable juice	8 ounces
Apple, sliced without skin	½ cup

Dinner

Crispy tofu★	1 serving
Black bean dip	2 tablespoons
Brown rice, medium grain	⅔ cup
Kale, chopped	½ cup
Carrots, glazed	½ cup
Banana	1 medium

Evening Snack

Fruit smoothie★	1 serving
Carrot sticks	½ cup

Basic Nutritional Summary

Calories: 2,042; protein: 101.36 grams; carbs: 290.47 grams; fat: 65.96 grams; saturated fat: 12.90 grams; cholesterol: 64.64 milligrams; sodium: 2,984.346 milligrams; fiber: 42.40 grams

15

Lower Carbohydrate Diet

This diet is lower in carbohydrates, higher in protein, and has the same amount of fat as the one in Chapter 14. If you need to lose weight, the higher level of protein can protect against muscle tissue loss. The lower level of fat can help to reduce the inflammation that can promote tumor growth. Because a carbohydrate is the only macronutrient to directly affect blood sugar levels, this diet can make it difficult for your tumor to steal your blood glucose.

Low-carbohydrate diets have different effects on different people. For many, eating carbohydrates just makes them hungry for more. They find a low-carb diet is the only way they can control their appetite and avoid strong cravings that result in carb binges and weight gain. For these people, this diet is the best choice. For others, *not* having carbohydrates causes cravings. Carbohydrates make them feel better and help them to control their appetite. A diet this low in carbs can be impossible for them to follow even though it is not as restrictive as most diets of this type. Listen to your body and let it be your guide.

If you have cut calories, you may lose more than one or two pounds in the first few weeks of this diet; but this is water loss and not fat loss. With less glucose coming in your muscle and liver cells will break open their glycogen piggy banks. As glucose rings cut off the glycogen molecules, water is formed and excreted in the urine. While this added weight loss is a good morale booster, the glycogen must be replaced, and water is needed for the reaction. This means that after a few months your body will adapt to the lower calorie level and the water weight will be regained. For a few weeks this can offset your fat loss and make it appear that your diet has stalled when it actually hasn't.

Keep in mind that all weight loss is not due to fat loss. Too often we think we have lost a pound of fat when we have really lost a combination of fat, water, and muscle. To protect your lean muscle tissue during weight loss, you must also exercise. (Read the section in Chapter 16 on weight loss for more information.) It's a good idea not to cut calories during the first month of this diet. Many people find they lose weight because they are no longer eating empty calories and refined and processed foods. Let your body adapt to the diet first. When you have cancer it is best to approach any changes gently and gradually.

A weight loss of 5 percent of your body weight is a red flag that something is wrong. Report it to your doctor. Also report any abrupt weight gain. Your body cannot lose or gain 5 pounds of fat or tissue overnight. Sudden changes such as these are due to water gain (edema) or loss.

Calculating Your Lower Carbohydrate Diet (45/25/30)

Follow these macronutrient guidelines:

- 45 percent carbohydrates (from whole, unprocessed foods)
- 25 percent protein (stressing beans, nuts, seeds, and fish)
- 30 percent fat (stressing monounsaturated and polyunsaturated fats and oils, with 7 percent or less from saturated fat)
- Less than 300 milligrams cholesterol

Next, look at the charts on fat grams and servings by caloric intake (Table 15.1) and carbohydrate grams and servings for each calorie level (Table 15.2). If your caloric intake is between calorie levels, move up or down toward the number that's closest to yours.

Once you have determined your caloric intake, use Table 15.3 to find the appropriate distribution of carbohydrates. This plan is based on three meals and three snacks. By distributing your carbohydrate servings evenly throughout the day, you avoid large spikes that might feed cancer cells and promote hunger. You can redistribute your carbohydrate servings to suit your own needs. For example, you might want more carbs for lunch than for dinner. Or you might want a 2-carb serving for a snack instead of one of a 1-carb serving. The only rule is to eat all six meals and snacks and not to go more than four hours without at least a whole-foods snack. (Chapter 13 has information on how to count carbs.)

Table 15.1 Fat Grams and Servings by Caloric Intake

CALORIES	FAT CALORIES	FAT GRAMS	FAT SERVINGS	SAT. FAT CAL	SAT. FAT GRAMS
1,400	420	47	9	98	11
1,600	480	53	11	112	12
1,800	540	60	12	126	14
2,000	600	67	13	140	16
2,200	660	73	15	154	17
2,400	720	80	16	168	19
2,600	780	87	17	182	20
2,800	840	93	19	196	22
3,000	900	100	20	210	23
3,200	960	107	21	224	25
3,400	1,020	113	23	238	26
3,600	1,080	120	24	252	28
3,800	1,140	127	25	266	30
4,000	1,200	133	27	280	31
4,200	1,260	140	28	294	33
4,400	1,320	147	30	308	34

Table 15.2 Carb Grams and Servings by Caloric Intake

CALORIES	CARB CALORIES	CARB GRAMS	CARB SERVINGS
1,200	540	135	9
1,400	630	158	11
1,600	720	180	12
1,800	810	203	14
2,000	900	225	15
2,200	990	248	17
2,400	1,080	270	18
2,600	1,170	293	20
2,800	1,260	315	21
3,000	1,350	338	23
3,200	1,440	360	24
3,400	1,530	383	26
3,600	1,620	405	27
3,800	1,710	428	29
4,000	1,800	450	30
4,200	1,890	473	32
4,400	1,980	495	33

Table 15.3 Carbohydrate Distribution by Caloric Intake (45/25/30)

CALORIES	BREAKFAST	SNACK	LUNCH	SNACK	DINNER	SNACK	TOTAL
1,400	2	1	3	1	3	1	11
1,600	2	1	3	1	4	1	12
1,800	3	1	4	1	4	1	14
2,000	3	1	4	1	5	1	15
2,200	4	1	4	1	5	2	17
2,400	4	1	4	1	6	2	18
2,600	5	1	5	1	6	2	20
2,800	5	1	5	2	6	2	21
3,000	6	1	6	2	6	2	23
3,200	6	2	6	2	6	2	24
3,400	6	2	7	2	7	2	26
3,600	6	2	7	2	7	3	27
3,800	7	2	7	2	8	3	29
4,000	7	2	8	2	8	3	30
4,200	7	3	8	2	9	3	32
4,400	8	3	8	2	9	3	33

Meal Plans for a Lower Carbohydrate Diet

The following meal plans are examples of the food choices you can make on this diet. We have included menus for both 1,600 calories and 2,000 calories (recipes for the entries marked with an asterisk can be found in Chapter 18). Your caloric and carb intake will vary from day to day because it is impossible to eat any percentage of calories precisely. Just adding an extra quarter-cup of oatmeal or a few more ounces of fish can change your CPF ratio. It is the average intake that counts.

Meal Plan for 1,600 Calories

Total calories: 1,613
CPF ratio: 46/25/29

Breakfast

Oatmeal (regular, quick, or instant)	1 cup
Milk, 1 percent	¾ cup
Blueberries, unsweetened	¼ cup
Walnuts, chopped	2 teaspoons
Tea or coffee (sweetened with a natural no- or low-calorie sweetener)	

Morning Snack

Walnuts, raw	1 ounce or 14 halves
Apple with skin	½ small

Lunch

Beef minestrone soup	1½ cups
A salad composed of the following:	
Tomato slice	2 half-inch slices
Onion, sweet	2 thin slices
Butter lettuce	2 cups
Light salad dressing of choice	1 tablespoon

Afternoon Snack

Cottage cheese, 1 percent	½ cup
Apple with skin	½ small

Dinner

Coho salmon, wild	5 ounces
Sweet potatoes, boiled with no salt and mashed	⅔ cup
Broccoli, chopped and tossed with juice and almonds	1 cup
Lemon juice	½ teaspoon
Almonds	1 teaspoon
Romaine hearts with radicchio and frisée	1 cup
(organic packaged salad mix)	
Olive oil dressing	1 tablespoon

Evening Snack

Yogurt, any flavor, nonfat	¾ cup

Basic Nutritional Summary

Calories: 1,613; protein: 102 grams; carbs: 191 grams; saturated fat: 54 grams; fat: 10 grams; cholesterol: 110 milligrams; sodium: 2,000 milligrams; fiber: 32 grams

Meal Plan for 2,000 Calories

Total calories: 1,968
CPF ratio: 46/22/32

Breakfast

Whole-grain bread, toasted	2 slices
Better butter with canola (for toast)	2 servings

Canola oil (for egg)	1 serving
Egg (combine with egg white and scramble in oil)	1 extra large
Egg white	1 large
Grapefruit sections packed in juice	1 cup

Morning Snack

Walnuts	1 ounce or 14 halves
Grapes	1 cup

Lunch

Sourdough pita pocket	1 pita
Mackerel salad★	1 cup
Green leaf lettuce, shredded	1 cup
Vegetable juice	6 ounces

Afternoon Snack

Apple, with skin	1 medium

Dinner

Coho salmon, wild	5 ounces
Sweet potatoes, mashed with no salt	⅔ cup
Salad greens with 3 tomato wedges	2 cups
Olive oil dressing	1 tablespoon
Broccoli, chopped, boiled, and drained	1 cup
Lemon juice	1 teaspoon
Almonds, sliced	1 teaspoon
Better butter with olive oil★	1 teaspoon

Evening Snack

Yogurt, nonfat	1 cup

Combine the following for a topping:

Almond meal	½ teaspoon
Ground flaxseed	½ teaspoon
Cinnamon	pinch

Basic Nutritional Summary

Calories: 1,967.87; protein: 111.97 grams; carbs: 232 grams; fat: 72 grams; saturated fat: 14 grams; cholesterol: 427 milligrams; sodium: 2,132 milligrams; fiber: 29 grams

16

Meal Planning When You Need to Gain or Lose Weight

Different types of treatment can call for different types of dietary changes. In this chapter we look at dietary recommendations for those who need to gain weight or lose weight.

What to Eat for Weight Gain

People can be thin for many reasons. Sometimes they are just naturally thin and have a high metabolism. Other times it is the result of dieting to keep weight at a socially acceptable level, a sign of malabsorption, or an indication of malnutrition. If you have trouble gaining or maintaining weight, see your doctor. You may have a thyroid problem or a disease that causes malabsorption, such as celiac disease.

While a thin, underweight body is much admired in the fashion magazines, it is often not strong enough to withstand the rigors of cancer and cancer treatment. Low weight means low levels of lean muscle tissue; low stores of fat for days when you cannot eat; and low stores of vitamins and minerals such as vitamin A, iron, and calcium.

If you are on a diet and eating less than 1,200 calories a day, stop. It is impossible to get all of the nutrients you need to prepare your body for treatment on this small amount of food. Remember, you are essentially preparing for war, and a storehouse of nutrients will be necessary to feed your immune soldiers.

On the other hand, don't just stuff yourself with anything that will fit in your mouth. Fried pies and Twinkies will cause a weight gain, but not the type you need. Junk food will put fat on you, but it will do nothing to build nutrient stores or lean muscle tissue.

Here are some tips for putting on weight in a healthy way:

- Eat five to six small meals a day rather than two to three large ones.
- If you cannot manage to eat all of the recommended vegetable servings, try juicing some of them.
- Foods that taste sweet should be eaten only on a full stomach.
- Cook meals that are appealing to the eye as well as the palate.
- Drink eight to ten glasses of water (preferably filtered) a day.
- Read the section in Chapter 11 on appetite loss and follow the guidelines there.

- Half an hour before meals, drink half a glass of water with a teaspoon of lemon juice to stimulate digestive juices.
- Exercise about half an hour before meals to stimulate your appetite.
- Don't drink fluids or soups before or with meals. They will fill you up and leave no room for foods that are nutrient dense.
- Make mealtimes a pleasant experience by relaxing beforehand, eating with friends or family, and creating a pleasant atmosphere at the table.
- If you do not gain weight, increase serving sizes.

A 5 percent weight loss from your normal weight is considered significant. Losing 10 percent of your normal weight should be considered a red flag. A 15 percent weight loss may lead to loss of appetite, fatigue, depression, and reduced ability to heal. If you do not obtain enough calories, proteins, and nutrients from this whole-foods diet and do not gain and maintain the proper weight, a nutritional supplement may be necessary. We prefer homemade protein shakes and a multivitamin to the canned liquid supplements.

Adding Nuts and Seeds to Your Diet

Nuts and seeds (Table 16.1) are rich in cancer-fighting and heart-healthy oils. Whenever you are hungry, a handful of nuts or seeds is a good choice for a snack because they are high-protein foods. Avoid nuts and seeds that are flavored, oiled, fried, or salted. Eat yogurt or chocolate-coated nuts in small amounts.

Table 16.1 Nuts and Seeds

Whole nuts and seeds
Tahini (sesame seed butter)
Hazelnut butter
Peanut butter (actually a legume butter)
Sunflower seed butter
Other nut and seed butters
Coconut milk
Almond milk
Other nut milks

Try these suggestions for incorporating nuts and seeds into your diet:

- Whole nuts and seeds. (One serving equals one medium handful.) Sprinkle seeds and crushed nuts on cereals, vegetables, and salads. Mix them with a small amount of dried fruit and eat as a snack or small meal. Use them to add a crunchy topping to casseroles.
- Nut and seed butters. (One serving equals 3 tablespoons.) Examples of nut butters include sesame seed butter (tahini), hazelnut butter, and peanut butter. To make your own nut butter, just add fresh unsalted nuts to a blender, food processor, or food grinder. Add sweeteners such as molasses or honey and seasonings such as cinnamon or nutmeg. Process until smooth.

  Savory nut butters can be made by adding garlic, onions, peppers, or other seasonings to the unsweetened nuts. Dilute nut butters with one of the oils in the next section and use as a salad dressing, or mix them with a little soy milk and use as a vegetable dip or sauce.

- Nut milks. Commercially available nut milks, which can be purchased in your local health food store and some grocery stores, include coconut milk, almond milk, and hazelnut milk. Nut milks can easily be made at home. Just add a handful of nuts to a blender with 1 cup of filtered water. Process until the water is milky in color. Strain to remove the fiber and store in the refrigerator. Nut milks can be sweetened with honey or molasses and then blended with fruit juice, dried fruit, soft whole fruit, yogurt, or soy milk to produce a calorie-rich meal shake. Store in the refrigerator where it will keep for four or five days.

When You Have Lost Weight: How Much Fat Do You Need?

If you have lost a lot of weight, your physician may want you to increase the amount of fats in your diet. This is because fats and other lipids are a concentrated source of energy. Carbohydrates and proteins each contribute 4 calories for every gram consumed. Fats contribute 9 calories per gram, more than double the other energy sources. Fats are also easily stored in the body, providing you with a backup source of energy for times when you cannot eat.

We suggest that these fats be high in the monounsaturated fatty acids or in omega-3 fatty acids like olive and canola oil. The fatty acids found in coconut milk are high in medium-chain triglycerides, which are easily absorbed with minimal digestion. The foods rich in monounsaturated fats will not only increase your caloric intake but will also aid in preventing metastasis and enhance your immune system. Keep salted foods to a minimum if sodium is not yet restricted. Salt can cause your body to hold water, and water weight can be mistaken for lean muscle weight gain. Polyunsaturated fats have been shown in animal and human studies to speed tumor growth and increase inflammation, and the sources of animal fats will tend to make your bodily fluids more acidic, which is more hospitable for tumor growth.

Sometimes radiation and chemotherapy cause temporary intestinal damage, which decreases your ability to digest fats. If this happens your stools will be frequent, bulky, and light in color, a condition called steatorrhea. Sometimes treatment affects the liver's ability to produce bile, which also results in fat malabsorption. Pancreatic enzymes may be reduced by treatment as well. If you suffer from malabsorption, we strongly suggest that you take a digestive enzyme supplement. (See Appendix A for names of suppliers.)

Each serving in Table 16.2 contains 5 grams of fat, which adds 45 calories to your diet. Thus, if you add four of these servings to one of the diets you will obtain an additional 20 fat grams or 180 fat calories. Add these foods two servings at a time until the weight loss stops.

What to Eat for Weight Loss

There is evidence that being overweight may increase the chances of cancer recurrence, especially with hormone-related cancers. In breast cancer patients who are overweight, weight loss can aid the healing process.

Table 16.2 Serving of High-Fat Foods

2 whole walnuts	1 tablespoon cashews
2 whole pecans	2–3 whole macadamia nuts
20 small peanuts	2 teaspoons peanut butter
10 small or 5 large olives	⅛ medium avocado
1 tablespoon pine nuts	1 tablespoon sunflower seeds
2 teaspoons pumpkin seeds	2 teaspoons tahini (sesame
1 teaspoon olive, canola,	seed butter)
safflower, or fish oil	2 tablespoons salad dressing
2 teaspoons canola	2½ teaspoons coconut milk
mayonnaise	2 fish oil capsules (1,000
2 tablespoons shredded	grams each)
coconut	½ cup firm tofu
¼ cup hummus with olive oil	1 ounce cooked Pacific
1 ounce cooked Atlantic	herring
mackerel	3 ounces cooked salmon
1 ounce cooked sablefish	2 ounces cooked trout
1 ounce cooked American	3 ounces cooked yellowtail
shad	1 egg (vegetarian fed)
3 ounces cooked whitefish	
3 ounces canned mackerel	
with bone	

But weight loss is easier said than done. Be realistic in setting goals. You do not have to aim for the often unrealistically low "desirable" weight. A moderate reduction of 10 to 15 percent has many of the same benefits with less chance of regaining the lost weight and less stress on the body and mind. If your diet has differed significantly from the high-carb diet in Chapter 14, it may be more prudent to start there.

We suggest you first try the high-carb diet without cutting back on calories. When people first eat a whole-foods diet, they often lose weight because of the greater volume of food. Instead of counting calories, count your carbohydrates, practice portion control, and concentrate on the quality of food. Focus on becoming healthier rather than thinner.

The only way to lose weight is to either take in fewer calories or burn more calories. For permanent weight loss you should not depend on one or the other but both. Take in fewer and burn more. You have probably heard this particular piece of advice so often you have tuned it out. Please tune it back in. It takes 3,500 calories to put on 1 pound. It takes burning an equal amount to lose 1 pound. Divide that 3,500 calories by seven days, and you get a decrease of 500 calories/day to lose approximately 4 pounds a month. Exceed this amount by much and you are no longer losing fat; you are losing water and muscle. Since muscle tissue burns more calories than fat cells, you are only sabotaging yourself when you burn muscle tissue for the sake of a quick weight loss. When the weight is regained, it is regained only as fat.

There is no way around this; it is how all weight loss diets work, no matter what diet promoters claim. Of course, the numbers are approximate, and it's impossible to know exactly how many calories a person is burning without expensive equipment. Not everyone will lose 1 pound of fat from burning 3,500 calories; some may need to burn more and some less. Some people burn calories more efficiently than others. We all know skinny gluttons who eat a large amount of food and never gain weight. We also know, or perhaps even are, people who gain weight on far fewer calories.

While on the higher carb diet, reevaluate your weight and caloric intake in two months. If you need to lose weight, then subtract the 500 calories and recalculate your diet plan. This amount of calories should result in a loss of 4 pounds a month. If you do not lose 1 or 2 pounds in a month, switch to the lower carb diet. Both diets are healthy, it is just a matter of which one is easiest for you to follow and which one helps you to control your hunger the best. Some people just do better on a lower carb diet.

Those on the lower carb diet will lose a few pounds more initially. This weight loss is really a water loss. Your body needs that water; it will acclimate to your new diet and eventually regain the fluid. Then the water weight gain will offset your fat tissue loss and you will think your diet is not working when it is. Or your muscle tissue gain will offset your fat tissue loss. Your muscles will be larger and your waist smaller, but your weight will be the same. For this reason a tape measure is often a better indicator of fat status than a scale.

Visceral Fat

Almost everyone who is overweight is also insulin resistant. This means your body is resistant to the effects of insulin—the hormone that controls blood sugar levels. When you are insulin resistant your blood sugar levels remain higher for longer after a meal. Insulin resistance is associated with a particular kind of fat: **visceral fat**. Some people are fat all over, and that fat tends to be confined to the layer of tissue just under the skin. Those who develop visceral fat tend to gain weight in their belly, around their internal organs, rather than just on top of the muscle layer. There is little fat on their arms, in their face, or on their legs, so sometimes they do not think of themselves as fat.

But it is this visceral fat that is associated with disease. It has been dubbed the "killer fat."

All adipose (fat) tissue secretes chemicals called adipokines. They help the brain with inventory, telling it how much fat is in storage. This allows the brain to control how much food enters the GI tract. Adipokines are also involved in appetite regulation in some way that is not yet understood. There appears to be one group of adipokines that wants you to gain weight and another group that doesn't. When the chemicals your fat cells secrete are balanced, you can eat until you are no longer hungry and not gain weight.

Visceral fat secretes more of the "eat more" factors and unbalances appetite regulation. The thinking part of your brain says, "I don't want to eat, I already weigh enough." But when energy intake falls, the "Chicken Little" part of your brain fears there is a food shortage. It runs around yelling, "The famine is coming! The famine is coming!" Survival instinct wins out over the thinking part of the brain; it makes you hungry and decreases the amount of energy it takes to run the body. Now you have more food coming in and less energy going out. Many people find that a lower carb diet helps them to lose visceral fat more easily than a higher carb diet.

Portion Control for Weight Control

In order to control your weight you must learn to control your portion sizes. Super-sizing is a major cause of being overweight, and portion control can help you control your weight. Here are some tips to help you with portion control.

- Buy yourself a set of measuring cups and spoons. For one month measure everything you eat. This will teach you how to estimate portion sizes.
- Most restaurants serve patrons double serving sizes. Eat half your entree and take the other half home for dinner or for lunch the next day.
- Stop serving meals family style. Rather than bringing food to the table and letting everyone fill their own plate, measure food out in the kitchen for the adults and allow no seconds.
- Let young children determine how much they want to eat. Adults often overestimate a child's energy needs and offer too much food. They need to learn how to listen to their body's needs. Encouraging your children to finish all the food on their plate is the same as encouraging them to overeat.
- Divide your plate into quarters. One quarter should be filled with a protein food, one with a whole-grain starch or starchy vegetable, and two quarters with vegetables. In at least one meal each day, half of the vegetables should be raw, as in a salad or raw vegetable appetizer. For dessert you should choose a serving of fruit. Most of all you should be able to see your plate under the food. If you like the sight of your plate piled high, start eating dinner on a luncheon plate. Of course, lunch should already be served on a luncheon plate.
- Start dinner with a low-calorie soup course. This can help to control your hunger and cause you to eat less for the rest of the meal.
- The need to crunch and chew is great, and lots of low-calorie foods meet this need. Lots of high-calorie foods do as well, and the challenge is to

make the switch. Find a snack that has the following four properties:

- Hard to eat (requires some effort to extract the food)
- Low fat, high volume
- Low calorie, high crunch
- High fiber (more than 6 grams)

Weight Reduction and Exercise

Regular exercise is one of the most important things you can do to improve glucose levels. It goes hand and hand with diet; your body needs both to keep healthy. There is no substitute for vigorous exercise just as there is no substitute for good food. The more active you are, the more weight you will lose. Weight-bearing exercise is important for building and keeping bone density to prevent osteoporosis. Exercise can even help to reduce insulin resistance and improve your sex life. It will also do wonders for your mental health. There is no better stress reliever than exercise.

Here are some tips to get you moving:

- **Walk 10,000 steps each day.** Get yourself a pedometer—a nifty and cheap little device that measures the number of steps you take each day. You will not be able to walk the full number of steps when you start, but add a hundred steps each day to slowly build toward your goal. The 10,000 Steps Program was put together by Shape Up America, a nonprofit organization dedicated to raising awareness of obesity as a health issue. See their webpage (http://shapeup.org) for more information.

- **Find an aerobic exercise you enjoy.** This includes running, jogging, biking, cross-country skiing, and even vigorous walking. If you don't like your exercise program, you won't stay with it, so put some thought into choosing activities.
- **Start slow and build up.** Gradually increase how long you spend exercising until you reach thirty to forty-five minutes at least three times a week. The higher your level of exercise, the greater your weight loss and health benefits. If you are obese or have been inactive for many years, it may take months before you can exercise this much. That's okay. Just take it slow and don't quit.
- **Be persistent and don't get discouraged.** Find a friend or join an exercise group to keep you motivated and committed to exercise.

Set Reasonable Weight Loss Goals

To measure your waist use a tape measure and be careful to hold it level. Measure your waist at the narrowest point on your torso, and touch the tape lightly to your skin, making it taut but not tight.

If you cannot find your natural waist, don't worry about getting an exact measurement. Under the folds, your waist is probably more than 40 inches. You may want to get an approximate measure to use for motivation. Nothing is as motivating as watching a waist shrink. Here are some reasonable weight loss goals:

- Reduce the circumference of your waist to less than 40 inches if you are a man and less than 35 inches if you are a woman.

- Reduce your body mass index to 30 or less.
- Have your hips be equal to or greater than your waist.

Your weight loss goal should be tackled 10 percent at a time. If you weigh 200 pounds, your first 10 percent will be 20 pounds. Your second 10 percent will be 18 pounds. After that first 10 percent your risk of developing many diseases falls substantially.

17

Meal Planning When You Are Undergoing Chemotherapy and Radiation

During chemotherapy and radiation the body is under stress. The guidelines in this chapter will help you give your body the resources it needs to cope.

What to Eat During Chemotherapy

Chemotherapy is recommended for patients whose cancers have the potential to spread, have spread, or are suspected of having spread to distant sites. Since chemotherapeutic agents are not limited to any particular area, they can circulate throughout your body, hopefully killing cancer cells that think they have escaped detection.

Nutrition Checklist for Chemotherapy

To Prevent or Slow Metastasis

• The oil in fish has EPA and DHA, which decrease cancer cells' ability to stick to blood vessels when they try to escape. During treatment, get these fats from fish, not supplements.

• Eat plenty of fiber-rich foods to keep blood sugar levels even. This will help to "starve" the glucose-hungry cancer cells.

• Decrease polunsaturated fats, which can increase inflammation.

To Protect Healthy Cells

• Take vitamin C and the other antioxidant nutrients—selenium, mixed tocopherols, and mixed carotenes—as part of an antioxidant supplement to provide protection from the free radicals used to kill cancer cells (friendly fire). These should be taken only after treatment starts, when cancer cells are vulnerable.

Many of the drugs used in chemotherapy interfere with cell division, because cancer cells divide faster than most normal tissue cells. When a drug interferes with cell division, the rapidly dividing cells are affected the most. This includes not only cancer cells, but the epithelial tissues that line the mouth, throat, and intestines. In the mouth, chemotherapy can cause mouth sores, tender or bleeding gums, sore throat, and difficulty swallowing. In the stomach it causes nausea and in the intestine, diarrhea.

- Coenzyme Q10 may protect the heart muscle from toxic drugs.
- Green tea contains strong antioxidants, and its tannins may prevent metastasis. Brew yourself a cup or two every day.

To Increase Detoxification of Chemotherapeutic Drugs
- Rice and wheat bran will increase the fecal excretion of drugs.
- Cruciferous vegetables will increase the production of the enzyme glutathione. Eat them liberally after starting treatment.
- N-acetylcysteine, an amino acid, will increase the enzyme glutathione.
- Silymarin (milk thistle seed extract) is well known for its ability to protect the liver from toxic chemicals.

The severity of chemotherapeutic side effects is related to the drug used, size of the dosage, length of treatment, and your individual response. Not everyone will have side effects. Some people breeze through the whole experience without giving it much thought. For others, chemotherapy becomes a full-time job.

Nutrition therapy during this time allows you to support healthy tissue while enhancing the toxicity to cancerous tissue. Cancer patients who have proper nutritional balance during chemotherapy have a better response and success rate with treatments. Specific recommendations for nutritionally related side effects appear in Chapter 11. Just add those dietary recommendations to the diet plan in this section. In addition, try these hints:

- Eat five to six small meals a day rather than two to three large ones.
- If you cannot manage to eat all of the recommended vegetable servings, try juicing some of them. You can have up to sixteen ounces of vegetable juice a day.
- Eat foods containing sugar only during meals.
- Cook meals that are appealing to the eye as well as the palate.
- You should get eight glasses of liquid from beverages, juices, soups, filtered water, or other foods each day.
- Always eat a protein-rich food with meals to keep blood sugar levels even, which controls your appetite better.
- Exercise according to your physician's instructions.

What to Eat During Radiation Therapy

Because of the side effects of radiation therapy, people undergoing such treatment should follow this diet to give the body extra protection and strength. Radiation therapy is used to treat localized tumors such as cancers of the skin, tongue, larynx, brain, breast, and cervix. Treatment exposes a defined area of tissue to ionizing radiation, damaging the DNA of all cells it reaches. The cancerous cells die from the injuries, but most normal cells will be able to repair themselves.

Gamma rays and x-rays are the two forms of photon energy used in external radiotherapy. They both have the same effect on cells and the same side effects. Cancerous cells can also be exposed to radiation using the technique of internal radiotherapy. Here radioactive implants are placed inside a tumor or body cavity. Internal radiation is often used for cancers of the tongue, uterus, and cervix. Radiation therapy can be used alone or in combination with chemotherapy or surgery.

Nutritional therapy during radiation therapy keeps the body nourished when side effects diminish appetite, protects the healthy cells from the effects of the radiation, makes the cancerous cells more vulnerable to the radiation, and speeds the healing of tissues damaged by radiation.

Radiation treatment can cause damage to the lining of the intestines, resulting in an inability to properly absorb protein, carbohydrates, fat, and other nutrients, as well as a loss of fluids and electrolytes. Add the specific recommendations for nutritionally related side effects from Chapter 11 to the diet plan found in this section. In addition, try these hints:

- Eat five or six small meals a day rather than two or three large ones.
- If you cannot manage to eat all of the recommended vegetable servings, try juicing some of them.
- Foods that taste sweet should be eaten only on a full stomach.

- Cook meals that are appealing to the eye as well as the palate.
- Drink eight to ten glasses of water (preferably filtered) a day.
- Don't drink fluids or soups before or with meals. They will fill you up and leave no room for foods that are nutrient dense.
- Make mealtimes a pleasant experience by relaxing before the meal, eating with friends or family, and creating a pleasant atmosphere at the table.
- If you do not gain weight, increase serving sizes. If this does not work, notify your physician immediately. Loss of weight can be caused by serious medical problems.
- Radiation treatment to the abdomen can cause a temporary inability to digest lactose. A lactose-free diet plan appears in the next section.

Nutrition Checklist for Radiation Therapy

- Glutamine may protect against radiation-induced enteritis.
- Vitamin B, niacin, vitamin C, and the other antioxidant nutrients—selenium, vitamin E, and mixed carotenes—protect healthy cells from radiation damage.
- Vitamin C and leafy green vegetables make cancer cells more vulnerable to radiation. Eat at least two servings of leafy green vegetables each day. These make good additions to juices.

- Radiation treatment to the abdomen can also make it difficult to digest and absorb high-fiber foods. Reduce raw fruits and vegetables and grain germs and brans.

If you do not obtain enough calories, proteins, and nutrients from this whole-foods diet and do not gain and maintain the proper weight, a nutritional supplement may be necessary.

Lactose-Free Diet Plan

Radiation and chemotherapy can sometimes damage the lining of the colon. This can cause a temporary lactose intolerance (Figure 17.1). Lactose is the sugar found in

Figure 17.1 Colon that is lactose intolerant

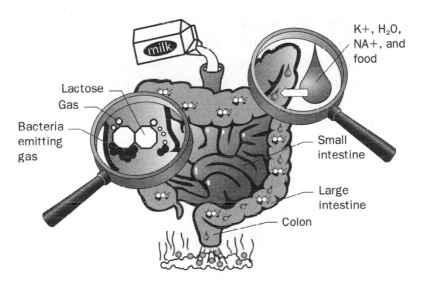

milk and milk products. It is digested in the small intestine by the enzyme lactase, which lies on top of the intestinal villi. When the villi are injured, lactase is reduced or no longer present. As a result the milk sugar is not digested and passes untouched into the colon. There, the undigested sugar pulls water into the colon, causing cramps and diarrhea. Some of the lactose becomes dinner for the many colonic bacteria, producing painful gas as an end product.

Do not confuse lactose intolerance with a milk allergy. Allergies are immune reactions to the *protein* in milk, whereas lactose intolerance involves the *sugar* in milk. Avoiding lactose will do you no good if your problem is a milk allergy.

As many as 30 million people in the United States lack sufficient quantities of lactase. But even those who have never experienced lactose intolerance before will have difficulty digesting dairy products during and after cancer treatments. This is the result of damage to the intestinal villi and the corresponding loss of the enzymes that lie on top of them. The condition is often temporary and fixes itself as the intestinal villi regrow.

If the intolerance is mild, you may simply need to supplement the missing enzyme, lactase, when you eat or drink a milk-containing product. This enzyme is available in pill, liquid, and capsule forms. Pretreated lactose-reduced milk and lactose-free milk also are available.

For more severe or persistent symptoms, eliminate lactose from your diet. The remainder of this section explains how.

Lactose Red Flags

You can eat everything listed in the diet plans from Chapters 14 and 15 except the following foods and beverages:

- Milk. Avoid milk from all species, including goat; skim, nonfat, 1 percent, 2 percent, and whole milk; powdered, dried, and instant nonfat or low-fat milk; acidophilus milk, buttermilk, yogurt, and any other cultured milk product; chocolate and other flavored milks; hot chocolate and cocoa; evaporated or condensed milk; half-and-half; and whipped cream, whipping cream, and clotted cream.
- Milk products. Do not eat or drink milk products, including low-fat, nonfat, and gourmet ice creams; ice milk, sherbet, frozen yogurt; milk shakes and malts; milk-based puddings; sour cream; butter and margarine; chocolate and cocoa; and yogurt–fruit juice beverages.
- Cheese. Do not eat any cheese, including all types of natural cheese, cream cheese, cottage cheese, processed cheese, artificial and fat-free cheeses, cheese sauce, and cheesecake.
- Any other products that contain lactose. To identify these products, read the ingredient labels. Among the products that often contain lactose are flavored coffee mixes; some nondairy creamers; Ovaltine; creamed vegetables and vegetables in butter or cream sauces; creamed soups; some sauces, such as white, hollandaise, cheese, or cream; chowders; some breads, muffins, cookies, and other bakery

items; some candies, such as toffee, butterscotch, caramels, fudge, and chocolates; dessert toppings such as chocolate syrup and hot fudge; desserts or entrees with a piecrust; French toast; some highly processed breakfast cereals, such as Total and Special K; flavored popcorns; omelets, soufflés, and quiches made with milk; some vitamins, food supplements, and medicines; and powdered sugar replacements such as Equal and Sweet 'n Low.

You may find that taking an enzyme replacement before eating or drinking a lactose-containing food is all you need to do to avoid symptoms. Lactose-free milk and milk products are available. This will be marked on the label. Ask for lactose-free products at your local supermarket or health food store. You may also use one of the following milk substitutes:

- Any product marked "lactose free"
- Any product marked "pareve"
- Lactic acid
- Lactate
- Lactoalbumin
- Fortified soy milk
- Nut milks such as cashew, coconut, or almond milks
- Rice milks such as Rice Dream

18

Recipes

Breakfast and Smoothies

Banana-Berry Breakfast Smoothie

This smoothie makes a protein-rich breakfast or other meal replacement. If you have an estrogen-related cancer, whey protein is an alternative to soy protein. Whey protein contains lactoferrin, which has antiviral, antibacterial, and anti-inflammatory properties, as well as cysteine and glutamine, amino acids necessary for production of the antioxidant glutathione.

Freeze the banana and/or blueberries, and you have a cold shake that soothes mouth sores or a sore throat.

2 scoops whey protein complex
1 medium banana
½ cup blueberries
4 ounces yogurt (nonfat) or milk (1 percent)

Place all ingredients in blender and process until smooth.

Makes one serving

Nutrition Information: 378 calories, 40 grams protein, 50 grams carbohydrates, 3 carb servings, 3.8 grams fat

Fruit Smoothie

This smoothie contains just two carbohydrate servings. If you need to gain or maintain weight, add the fresh flaxseed oil to the recipe. If you need more protein, add another scoop of whey protein.

½ cup strawberries
6 ounces plain nonfat yogurt
½ medium banana
1 scoop whey protein
1 tablespoon flaxseed oil (optional)

Place all ingredients in blender and process until smooth. Using frozen fruit results in a thicker, icier smoothie.

Makes one serving

Nutrition Information: 231 calories, 24 grams protein, 33 grams carbohydrates, 2 carb servings, 1.4 grams fat

With 1 tablespoon flaxseed oil: 351 calories, 24 grams protein, 33 grams carbohydrates, 2 carb servings, 15.5 grams fat

With an additional scoop of protein: 441 calories, 41 grams protein, 35 grams carbohydrates, 2 carb servings, 16.4 grams fat

Lunches and Dinners

Red Bean and Beef Stew

This recipe is a good way to introduce beans to a beef eater. We strongly suggest consuming only organic produce and grass-fed beef, if you must absolutely have beef in your diet. Grass-fed beef is lower in saturated fat and higher in omega-3 fatty acids. Tempeh, another soybean product, and chicken can be substituted for the beef.

> *1½ cups sliced yellow onion*
> *2 teaspoons extra-virgin olive oil*
> *1 15-ounce can organic kidney beans, drained and rinsed*
> *1 cup beef broth*
> *1 cup salsa*
> *½ cup organic tomato puree*
> *1 teaspoon chili powder*
> *1 teaspoon ground basil*
> *1 teaspoon ground oregano*

½ teaspoon curry powder
½ teaspoon red pepper flakes
1 teaspoon extra-virgin olive oil
6 ounces grass-fed eye of round roast cube steak, cut into bite-sized pieces

1. Add 2 teaspoons olive oil to large saucepan and sauté onions until brown.
2. Add drained and rinsed kidney beans, beef broth, salsa, tomato puree, and spices to the onions.
3. Cook vegetable mixture over medium heat for 5 minutes.
4. While the vegetables are cooking, add 1 teaspoon olive oil to a wok or pan and stir-fry beef until cooked through.
5. Divide beef equally between two bowls. Ladle equal amounts of bean mixture over beef and serve immediately.

Makes two 2-cup servings

Nutrition Information: 400 calories, 33 grams protein, 43 grams carbohydrates, 3 carb servings, 11 grams fat

Sea Vegetable Soup

This soup contains shiitake mushrooms, sea vegetables, garlic, and miso—all ingredients with medicinal properties. Have it at least once a week while you're receiving cancer treatment. It will help to replenish potassium and sodium due to fluid loss.

6 cups filtered water
6 whole dried medium shiitake mushrooms
2 6-inch pieces of wakame (seaweed)
1 teaspoon canola oil
1 medium onion, diced
2 tablespoons minced fresh ginger
3 medium cloves garlic, chopped
2 tablespoons low-sodium soy sauce
2 tablespoons vegetable stock powder
2 tablespoons chopped dulse (seaweed)
1 tablespoon red miso
1 tablespoons rice vinegar
3 tablespoons thinly sliced green onions

1. Heat 2 cups of the water until warm.
2. Rinse mushrooms and wakame and add to warm water. Soak until soft, about 10 minutes. Put soaking water aside.
3. Cut off and discard mushroom stems. Cut mushrooms into thin slices and chop wakame into 1-inch pieces. Return wakame pieces and mushroom slices to water.
4. In a large pot, sauté onion in canola oil until browned, stirring frequently. Add ginger and garlic to pot and continue to sauté for another minute.
5. Add wakame, mushrooms, and soaking water to pot along with the rest of the water, soy sauce, and vegetable stock.
6. Bring to a boil and add chopped dulse.
7. Reduce heat and simmer uncovered for 10 minutes.

8. Stir in miso and rice vinegar.
9. Pour into bowls and sprinkle green onions on top.

Makes four 1½-cup servings

Nutrition Information: 60 calories, 4 grams protein, 10 grams carbohydrates, ½ carb serving, 3 grams fat

Crispy Tofu

Substitute crispy tofu for the beef in the preceding recipe or top with a homemade salsa.

> 1 pound firm tofu
> 3 tablespoons whole-wheat flour
> 2 tablespoons garlic powder
> 1 teaspoon sea salt
> 1 teaspoon black pepper
> 1 teaspoon olive oil

1. Cut tofu into 1-inch cubes or into thin slices for a sandwich.
2. Combine dry ingredients in a bowl with a tight lid. Add tofu, cover, and shake.
3. Heat oil in a nonstick skillet.
4. Add coated tofu and cook over medium heat, turning often, until golden brown.

Makes four servings

Nutrition Information: 200 calories, 19.3 grams protein, 10.3 grams carbohydrates, ½ carb serving, 11.2 grams fat

Mackerel Salad

Due to concerns about heavy-metal contamination, the Food and Drug Administration and Environmental Protection Agency recommends that women who may become pregnant, pregnant women, nursing mothers, and young children avoid certain fish. That list includes fresh tuna, swordfish, shark, tilefish, king mackerel, and canned albacore tuna. Canned mackerel or canned salmon make good substitutes for tuna. Canned mackerel is a good source of the omega-3 fatty acids, EPA, and DHA, while canned tuna is not. Make one fish meal a week from canned mackerel.

This is a versatile salad. You can fill a mini (4-inch diameter) pita pocket with ¼ cup of salad, making a good snack food with only 214 calories, 15 grams carbohydrates, and 1 carb serving. Or you can stuff tomatoes, cucumbers, or bell peppers with half a cup of salad. Spread a serving on whole-grain bread for a sandwich, gently heat one serving and stuff into half of a baked Yukon gold potato, or toss a serving of salad with pasta and serve hot or cold.

> 1 14-ounce can mackerel, drained
> ¼ cup diced celery
> ¼ cup chopped green onions
> 3 tablespoons nonfat plain yogurt
> 2 tablespoons canola mayonnaise
> 1 tablespoon fresh/frozen lemon juice
> ¼ teaspoon coarsely ground pepper

1. Combine ingredients, including bone and skin of mackerel.

Makes about three ½-cup servings

Nutrition Information: 275 calories, 29 grams protein, 2.5 grams carbohydrates, 0 carb servings, 15.6 grams fat

Sides

Garlic and Cheese Dip

The great taste of cheese without the calories. Garlic is like a pharmacy in a clove.

> *½ cup unflavored nonfat yogurt*
> *1 teaspoon garlic, minced*
> *¼ teaspoon salt*
> *1½ cups nonfat or low-fat cottage cheese*

1. Add all ingredients to food processor or blender and process until smooth.
2. Serve with raw veggies as a dip or as a substitute for mayonnaise in salads. Store unused portions in refrigerator.

Makes about eight ½-cup servings

Nutrition Information: 39 calories, 6 grams protein, 2.8 grams carbohydrates, 0 carb servings, 0.4 grams fat

Yogurt Salsa

Salsa is a combination of chiles, tomatoes, and spices. It is an ancient dish, and its origins can be traced all the way back to the ancient Aztecs, Mayans, and Incas. More recently the term has widened to include combinations of fruit and spices. Salsa is a rich source of antioxidants. It provides nutrition while stimulating the taste buds and appetite. Most of all, we like salsa because it is so versatile. When fatigue prevents you from cooking appetizing meals, salsa can dress up (and spice up) an otherwise bland vegetable dish, chicken breast, or grilled fish fillet. Here are some ideas for using salsa:

- Toss salsa with canned mackerel for a quick fish salad
- Toss salsa with a baby lettuce mix for a green salad.
- Serve salsa as a vegetable dip.
- Top a cup of canned beans with salsa.
- Instead of plain rice, mix cooked rice with salsa and heat gently.
- Top a baked Yukon gold potato with salsa.
- Stir-fry firm tofu cubes in olive oil until crispy and top with salsa.

In this and the next recipe, we use plum tomatoes because they have less juice to thin the salsa and have a firmer flesh that holds its shape. One quarter-cup serving of salsa adds almost no carbohydrates or carb servings to your meal plan, so you can enjoy it with low-carb veggies anytime you want.

In Yogurt Salsa, the quercetin in the onions and lycopene in the tomatoes make it a true health food. If the tissue in your mouth is inflamed, eliminate the jalapeño.

1 pound ripe plum tomatoes (about 4 large), peeled
1 medium onion, peeled and cut into eighths
1 jalapeño pepper, seeded and chopped
¼ cup plain low-fat yogurt
½ cup chopped fresh cilantro
¼ teaspoon coursely ground fresh pepper

1. Cut tomatoes in half and gently squeeze to remove seeds and excess juice.
2. Add all ingredients to food processor and chop coarsely using the pulse button.
3. Chill for several hours to mingle flavors.

Makes about eight ½-cup servings

Nutrition Information: 18 calories, 1 gram protein, 9.7 grams carbohydrates, ½ carb serving, 0.10 grams fat

Mild Salsa

This recipe calls for bell peppers instead of hot peppers, making it a mild but flavorful alternative for those with sore mouths or throats. The flaxseed oil makes it very anti-inflammatory. Each half-cup serving adds about 100 calories to a meal for those who are trying to gain or maintain weight. It contains no carb servings to elevate glucose.

1½ cups raw plum tomatoes, peeled and chopped
1 cup avocado, peeled and chopped
¾ cup sweet red bell pepper, chopped
¼ cup minced red onion
2 tablespoons chopped fresh cilantro

1 tablespoon red wine vinegar
2 tablespoons flaxseed oil

1. Cut tomatoes in half and gently squeeze to remove seeds and excess juice.
2. Add all ingredients except oil to food processor and chop coarsely using the pulse button.
3. Add flaxseed oil and chill for several hours to mingle flavors.

Makes about seven ½-cup servings

Nutrition Information: 100 calories, 1.14 grams protein, 5.4 grams carbohydrates, 0 carb servings, 8.2 grams fat

Natural Laxatives

Constipation is a common problem in cancer patients. It has two underlying causes: lack of fiber and a sleepy colon. Even healthy Americans do not eat enough fiber. When your appetite decreases because of cancer therapy, so does the fiber content in your diet. This type of constipation responds to fiber supplements (laxatives). The soluble fiber they contain not only adds bulk to feces but feeds both the cells that line the colon and the bacteria that grow on them. The bacteria then add their bodies to the fecal mass.

The sole ingredient in the original unflavored Metamucil is ground psyllium seed, a natural and beneficial food. Pass on the artificial fiber supplements. Real fiber does more than just pass through the body; it nourishes your colon.

A sleepy colon occurs when opioid pain medications decrease the muscle movements that propel food through the digestive tract. This means that waste matter stays in the colon longer than it should, losing water and becoming hard and dry. The result can be an impaction and a trip to the emergency room for it to be manually removed. A fiber laxative alone will not prevent this kind of constipation; you need a stimulant laxative that will wake up your colon and force it to get going.

If you take any kind of opiate—such as codeine, morphine, oxycodone, methadone, fentanyl, or hydromorphone—for pain control, you *must* be on some sort of bowel control program or risk fecal impaction. Ask your doctor what is right for you.

Fruit Spread

In addition to being delicious, this fruit spread contains natural stimulants. The original recipe comes from a doctor who treats chronic pain patients. Unlike other laxative fruit spreads, this one contains senna, a stimulant laxative.

The recommended starting dose is 1 to 2 tablespoons a day. You can eat the spread right out of the freezer or put it on bread for a nighttime snack that will produce results in the morning. Increase or decrease the amount of spread to suit your needs.

> *4 ounces senna tea leaves (you can buy them online or find them at a health food store)*
> *1 pound prunes (dried plums)*
> *1 pound raisins*

1 pound figs
1 cup brown sugar
1 cup lemon juice (frozen or fresh)

1. Make senna "tea." Rinse teapot with boiling water. Put leaves in the bottom and pour about 2½ cups actively boiling water over them. Hot water will not do, only boiling will draw all of the stimulant out of the leaves. Steep tea for a full 5 minutes.
2. Pour tea through a tea strainer to remove leaves. Add 2 cups of tea to large pot.
3. Add prunes, raisins, and figs to pot and mix with tea.
4. Bring fruit mixture to a boil, reduce heat, and continue to cook for 5 minutes.
5. Remove pot from heat and mix in sugar and lemon juice. Allow to cool.
6. Using a blender or food processor, blend fruit until smooth.
7. Store mixture in freezer. The high sugar content will not allow fruit mix to freeze but will help to preserve it.

Variation: Dissolve 2 tablespoons spread in ½ cup warm water. Add 4 to 6 ounces cold water and immediately stir in 1 teaspoon of unflavored ground psyllium seed. Drink immediately (it will get thick if it stands). This drink provides both stimulant and bulk laxatives.

Makes one serving

Nutrition Information: 24 calories, 0.2 grams protein, 6.4 grams carbohydrates, 0 carb servings, 0.04 grams fat

Power Pudding

The "power" in this recipe comes from insoluble fiber in the wheat bran, sorbitol in the apple juice, and prune juice. This recipe came from a study published in the June 1995 issue of *Home Healthcare Nurse*. Dubbed "Power Pudding," it was shown to be effective at restoring bowel control in a group of homebound elderly patients. Basically this is a natural fiber laxative that works as a bulking agent. The recommended dose is ¼ cup of pudding with breakfast.

½ cup applesauce
½ cup prune juice
½ cup stewed prunes (packaged)
½ cup wheat bran flakes
½ cup whipped topping
½ teaspoon cinnamon

1. Using food processor or blender, process ingredients until the mixture has a smooth puddinglike consistency.
2. Cover and store in refrigerator. Pudding keeps for one week.

Makes ten ¼-cup servings

Nutrition Information: 45 calories, 0.6 gram protein, 10.6 grams carbohydrates, ½ carb serving, 0.8 gram fat

Better Butter

Even though this product must be stored in the refrigerator, it stays soft so it can be used straight out of the fridge.

1 part softened butter
1 part canola oil, extra-virgin olive oil, or flaxseed oil

Add butter and oil to food processor and mix. Store in the refrigerator. Serving size is 1 teaspoon.

Nutrition Information: 32 calories, 0.01 gram protein, 0 grams carbohydrate, 0 carb servings, 3.6 grams fat

Appendix A

Resources for Patients and Families

Information on Cancer and Cancer Programs

Cancer Information Services (CIS)
http://cis.nci.nih.gov
Phone: 800-4-CANCER (800-422-6237)

Information from the U.S. National Cancer Institute, including access to links, press releases, and publications, is available here.

National Cancer Institute (NCI)
cancer.gov/cancertopics/factsheet

This is home to the NCI fact sheet collection, which includes information on a variety of cancer topics. Fact sheets are updated and revised frequently based on the latest cancer research.

American Cancer Society (ACS)

cancer.org

Phone: 800-ACS-2345 (800-227-2345)

The ACS is a nonprofit organization offering a variety of services to patients and their families. This website is a treasure trove of information. You can look up information about specific types of cancer, find a clinical trial, and search for support groups near your home. ACS programs include the Man to Man Program for men with prostate cancer and the Reach for Recovery program for women with breast cancer.

CancerConsultants.com

http://cancerconsultants.com

This website is dedicated to providing comprehensive prevention and treatment information, daily news, and listings of clinical trials for cancer patients and their families.

Look Good . . . Feel Better (LGFB)

lookgoodfeelbetter.org

Phone: 800-395-LOOK (800-395-5665)

This is a nonprofit organization to help offset appearance-related changes from cancer treatment. It sponsors workshops, one-on-one sessions, and a free self-help kit for patients who do not have local access to LGFB.

Cancer Survivors Network

acscsn.org

Cancer survivors, families, and friends can share their experiences, strength, and hope at this bulletin board and chat room site.

National Center for Complementary and Alternative Medicine (NCCAM)
nccam.nih.gov

Information on alternative medicine is available here.

Products

Medium-chain triglycerides—you can purchase MCT products online from the following sites:
mothernature.com
vrp.com

Enova oil—you can purchase Enova oil in your local supermarket or go to the website at enovaoil.com.

Stevia—steviasmart.com. Stevia is a noncaloric natural sweetener that does not affect glucose or insulin levels.

Grass-fed beef—to learn more about the benefits of grass-fed beef we suggest that you visit the website for the California Food & Fiber Future Grant and the California State University, Chico Agricultural Research Initiative at csuchico.edu/agr/grassfedbeef.

The Sierra Club's website also has information on grass-fed beef at sierraclub.org/e-files/grassfed.asp.

To learn how you can buy grass-fed beef online, try these websites:
meatshopoftacoma.com
grasslandbeef.com
nfrnaturalbeef.com
diamondorganics.com

Supplements

Vitamin Research Products
Carson City, NV 89706
800-877-2447

An excellent source of several well-balanced vitamin and mineral, MCT oil, fish oil, and protein supplements. You can buy via mail-order, telephone, or the website (vrp .com).

The Vitamin Shoppe
vitaminshoppe.com

A wide variety of products is available, including Designer Whey Natural (a whey protein powder), flaxseed oil, and coconut oil.

Enzymes

Metazyme nonanimal digestive enzymes—call Metagenics Corporation at 800-338-3948 to find out who sells these products in your area.

Beano—beanogas.com. This product prevents flatulence from legumes and vegetables. It is available in grocery stores and pharmacies, or you can order it at online pharmacies and stores such as drugstore.com, walgreens.com, and amazon.com.

Similase—you can order this highly concentrated digestive enzyme formula online at shopping.msn.com, ritecare .com, or naturalnutritionals.com.

Lactaid—lactaid.com. This enzyme digests lactose or milk sugar for those with permanent or temporary lactose intolerance. It is available at grocery stores and pharmacies.

Mail-Order and Online Resources

Bob's Red Mill Natural Foods
5209 SE International Way
Milwaukie, OR 97222
bobsredmill.com
800-349-2173; fax 503-653-1339

Business hours: 8 A.M. to 5 P.M. (Pacific Time), M–F.

Bob's Red Mill is a source of a wide variety of common and hard-to-find grains. You can choose from a number of breakfast grain mixtures. Other products include flaxseed and other organic grains and seeds, stone-ground whole-grain products, gluten-free products, beans and soup mixes, dried fruit, and herbs and spices.

Arrowhead Mills
arrowheadmills.com
800-434-4246

Business hours: 7 A.M. to 5 P.M. (Mountain Time), M–F.

This is a good source for whole grains, legumes, and nuts and seeds, including organic flaxseed. All Arrowhead flours are certified organic.

Spectrum Organic Products, Inc.
5341 Old Redwood Highway, Suite 400
Petaluma, CA 94954
spectrumorganics.com

Here's a source for organic oils, fish oil, flaxseed, salad dressings, and canola and flaxseed mayonnaise. Order online, use the online store finder to locate a vendor near you, or look in your local health food store or grocery store.

Imagine Foods
imaginefoods.com

A source for organic broths, stocks, and soups.

Harvest Direct Inc.
Box 4514
Decatur, IL 62521-4514
800-835-2867

Business hours are 9 A.M. to 6 P.M. (Eastern Time), M–F.

This company sells textured vegetable protein.

Thorne Research, Inc.
thorne.com
800-228-1966

Business hours are 9 A.M. to 5 P.M. (Pacific Time), M–F.

Thorne's vitamin, mineral, and encapsulated products are of high quality and are sold only through health professionals. Call for the names of practitioners in your area who carry these products. Among the offerings appropriare for those undergoing cancer treatment are digestive enzymes, bioflavonoids, black currant oil, vitamins, minerals, and multivitamins.

Other Websites to Visit

For more information on nutrition and Maureen Keane's books, go to her website at http://keanenutrition.com.

For further information about the risks of methylmercury in fish and shellfish, call the U.S. Food and Drug Administration's food information line toll-free at 888-SAFEFOOD (888-723-3366) or visit their Food Safety website at cfsan.fda.gov/seafood1.html.

The "Official Website of the Glycemic Index and GI Database" at the University of Sydney has a free searchable database at glycemicindex.com.

Appendix B

Suggested Reading Materials

Books About Cancer

Austin, Steven, and Cathy Hitchcock. *Breast Cancer: What You Should Know About Prevention, Diagnosis, and Treatment.* Rocklin, CA: Prima Publishing, 1994.

Rosenberg, Steven A., and John M. Barry. *The Transformed Cell: Unlocking the Mysteries of Cancer.* New York: G. P. Putnam's Sons, 1992.

Books on Nutrition

Haas, Elson M. *Staying Healthy with Nutrition: The Complete Guide to Diet and Nutritional Medicine.* Berkeley, CA: Celestial Arts, 1992.

Keane, Maureen B., and Daniella Chace. *Grains for Better Health*. Rocklin, CA: Prima Publishing, 1994.

Murray, Michael. *The Healing Power of Herbs: The Enlightened Person's Guide to the Wonders of Medicinal Plants*. Rocklin, CA: Prima Publishing, 1991.

Murray, Michael, and Joseph Pizzorno. *The Encyclopedia of Natural Medicine*. Rocklin, CA: Prima Publishing, 1990.

Quillin, Patrick. *Beating Cancer with Nutrition*. With Noreen Quillin. Tulsa, OK: The Nutrition Times Press, 1994.

Books for Professionals

Quillin, Patrick, and Michael Williams, eds. *Adjuvant Nutrition in Cancer Treatment: 1992 Symposium Proceedings*. Arlington Heights, IL: Cancer Treatment Research Foundation, 1994.

Werbach, Melvyn R. *Nutritional Influences on Illness III*. Tarzana, CA: Third Line Press Inc., 1995.

Appendix C

References

Chapter 5

Brand-Miller JC. Glycemic load and chronic disease. *Nutr Rev.* 2004;61(5 Pt 2):S49–S55.

Folsom AR, Anderson KE, Sweeney C, Jacobs DR Jr. Diabetes as a risk factor for death following endometrial cancer. *Gynecol Oncol.* 2004;94(3):740–745.

Krone CA, Ely JT. Controlling hyperglycemia as an adjunct to cancer therapy. *Integr Cancer Ther.* 2005; 4(1):25–31.

Silvera SA, Rohan TE, Jain M, Terry PD, Howe GR, Miller AB. Glycaemic index, glycaemic load and risk of endometrial cancer: A prospective cohort study. *Public Health Nutr.* 2005;8(7):912–919.

Wei EK, Ma J, Pollak MN, Rifai N, Fuchs CS, Hankinson SE, Giovannucci E. A prospective study of C-peptide, insulin-like growth factor-I, insulin-like growth factor binding protein-1, and the risk of colorectal cancer in women. *Cancer Epidemiol Biomarkers Prev.* 2005;14(4):850–855.

Chapter 6

Barber MD. Cancer cachexia and its treatment with fish-oil-enriched nutritional supplementation. *Nutrition.* 2001;17:751–755.

Bruera E, Strasser F, Palmer JL, et al. Effect of fish oil on appetite and other symptoms in patients with advanced cancer and anorexia/cachexia: A double-blind, placebo-controlled study. *J Clin Oncol.* 2003;21: 129–134.

Das UN, Ramadevi G, Rao KP, et al. Prostaglandins can modify gamma-radiation and chemical induced cytotoxicity and genetic damage in vitro and in vivo. *Prostaglandins Dec.* 1989;38(6):689–716.

Kimoto Y, Tanji Y, Taguchi T, et al. Antitumor effect of medium-chain triglyceride and its influence on the self-defense system of the body. *Cancer Detect Prev.* 1998;22:219–224.

Maki C, et al. Consumption of diacylglycerol oil as part of a mildly reduced-energy diet enhances loss of body weight and fat compared with a triacylglycerol control oil. *Am J Clin Nutr.* 2002;76:1230–1236.

Melanson SF, Lewandrowski EL, Flood JG, Lewandrowski KB. Measurement of organochlorines in commercial over-the-counter fish oil preparations: Implications for dietary and therapeutic recommendations for omega-3 fatty acids and a review of the literature. *Arch Pathol Lab Med*. 2005;129(1):74–77.

Ochoa JJ, Farquharson AJ, Grant I, Moffat LE, Heys SD, Wahle KWJ. Conjugated linoleic acids (CLAs) decrease prostate cancer cell proliferation: Different molecular mechanisms for cis-9, trans-11 and trans-10, cis-12 isomers. *Carcinogenesis*. 2004;25:1185–1191.

Siezen CL, van Leeuwen AI, Kram NR, Luken ME, van Kranen HJ, Kampman E. Colorectal adenoma risk is modified by the interplay between polymorphisms in arachidonic acid pathway genes and fish consumption. *Carcinogenesis*. 2005;26(2):449–457.

Tisdale MJ, Brennan RA. A comparison of long-chain triglycerides and medium-chain triglycerides on weight loss and tumour size in a cachexia model. *Br J Cancer*. 1988;58:580–583.

Tisdale MJ, Dhesi JK. Inhibition of weight loss by omega-3 fatty acids in an experimental cachexia model. *Cancer Res*. 1990;50:5022–5026.

Watanabe S, Katagiri K, Onozaki K, et al. Dietary docosahexaenoic acid but not eicosapentaenoic acid suppresses lipopolysaccharide-induced interleukin-1 beta mRNA induction in mouse spleen leukocytes. *Prostaglandins Leukot Essent Fatty Acids*. 2000;62(3):147–152.

Yang M, Cook ME. Dietary conjugated linoleic acid decreased cachexia, macrophage tumor necrosis factor-alpha production, and modifies splenocyte cytokines production. *Exp Biol Med* 2003;228:51–58.

Chapter 7

Cangiano C, Laviano A, Meguid MM, et al. Effects of administration of oral branched-chain amino acids on anorexia and caloric intake in cancer patients. *J Natl Cancer Inst.* 1996;88:550–552.

Chapter 8

Abdel-Latif MM, Raouf AA, Sabra K, Kelleher D, Reynolds JV. Vitamin C enhances chemosensitization of esophageal cancer cells in vitro. *J Chemother.* 2005; 17(5):539–549.

Benner SE, et al. Regression of oral leukoplakia with alpha-tocopherol: A community clinical oncology program chemoprevention study. *J Natl Cancer Inst.* 1993; 85(1):44.

Bouillon R, Moody T, Sporn M, Barrett JC, Norman AW. *J Steroid Biochem Mol Biol.* 2005 Oct; 97(1-2): 3-5. NIH deltanoids meeting on vitamin D and cancer—conclusion and strategic options.

de Vries N, Snow GB. Relationships of vitamins A and E and beta-carotene serum levels to head and neck cancer patients with and without second primary tumors. *Eur Arch Otorhinolaryngol.* 1990;247(6):368–370.

Eskelson CD, et al. Modulation of cancer growth by vitamin E and alcohol. *Alcohol.* 1993;28(1):117–125.

Giovannucci E. The epidemiology of vitamin D and colorectal cancer: Recent findings. *Curr Opin Gastroenterol.* 2006;22(1):24–29.

Kaya E, Keskin L, Aydogdu I, Kuku I, Bayraktar N, Erkut MA. Oxidant/antioxidant parameters and their relationship with chemotherapy in Hodgkin's lymphoma. *J Int Med Res.* 2005;33(6):687–692.

Kim KN, Pie JE, Park JH, Park YH, Kim HW, Kim MK. Retinoic acid and ascorbic acid act synergistically in inhibiting human breast cancer cell proliferation [electronic version]. *J Nutr Biochem.* 2005, Nov. 15.

Mehta RR, et al. Significance of plasma retinol binding protein levels in recurrence of breast tumors in women. *Oncology.* 1987;44(6):350–355.

Ngah WZ, et al. Effect of tocotrienols on hepatocarcinogenesis induced by 2-acetylaminofluorene in rats. *Am J Clin Nutr.* 1991;53(4 Suppl):1076S–1081S.

Santamaria LA, Santamaria AB. Cancer chemoprevention by supplemental carotenoids and synergism with retinol in mastodynia treatment. *Med Oncol Tumor Pharmacother.* 1990;7(2–3):153–167.

Schwartz J, Shklar G. The selective cytotoxic effect of carotenoids and alpha-tocopherol on human cancer cell lines in vitro. *J Oral Maxillofac Surg.* 1992;50(4): 367–373.

Sonn GA, Aronson W, Litwin MS. Impact of diet on prostate cancer: A review. *Prostate Cancer Prostatic Dis.* 2005;8(4):304–310.

Stahelin HB, et al. Plasma antioxidant vitamins and subsequent cancer mortality in the 12-year follow-up of the prospective Basel study. *Am J Epidemiol.* 1991; 133(8):766–775.

Stich HF, et al. Remission of precancerous lesions in the oral cavity of tobacco chewers and maintenance of the protective effect of beta-carotene or vitamin A. *Am J Clin Nutr.* 1991;53(1 Suppl):298S–304S.

van Bokhorst-de van der Schueren MA. Nutritional support strategies for malnourished cancer patients. *Eur J Oncol Nurs.* 2005;9(Suppl 2):S74–S83.

Part II

Caan BJ, Coates AO, Slattery ML, et al. Body size and the risk of colon cancer in a large case-control study. *Int J Obes Relat Metab Disord.* 1998;22(2):178–184.

Daniele B, Perrone F, Gallo C, et al. Oral glutamine in the prevention of fluorouracil induced intestinal toxicity: A double blind, placebo controlled, randomised trial. *Gut.* 2001;48:28–33.

Ferrandiz ML, Alcaraz MJ. Anti-inflammatory activity and inhibition of arachidonic metabolism by flavonoids. *Agents Actions.* 1991;32(3–4):283–288.

Frydoonfar HR, McGrath DR, Spigelman AD. Sulforaphane inhibits growth of a colon cancer cell line. *Colorectal Dis.* 2004;6(1):28–31.

Frydoonfar HR, McGrath DR, Spigelman AD. The effect of indole-3-carbinol and sulforaphane on a prostate cancer cell line. *ANZ J Surg.* 2003;73(3):154–156.

Goodman MT, Hankin JH, Wilkens LR, et al. Diet, body size, physical activity, and the risk of endometrial cancer. *Cancer Res.* 1997;57(22):5077–5085.

Haapapuro ER, Barnard ND, Simon M. Review—Animal waste used as livestock feed: Dangers to human health. *Prev Med.* 1997;26(5 Pt 1):599–602.

Huang Z, Hankinson SE, Cloditz GA, et al. Dual effects of weight and weight gain on breast cancer risk. *JAMA.* 1997;278(17):1407–1411.

Inui A. Cancer anorexia-cachexia syndrome: Current issues in research and management. *CA Cancer J Clin.* 2002;52:72–91.

Jackson SJ, Singletary KW. Sulforaphane inhibits human MCF-7 mammary cancer cell mitotic progression and tubulin polymerization. *J Nutr.* 2004;134(9): 2229–2236.

Jakovljevic J, Touillaud MS, Bondy ML, Singletary SE, Pillow PC, Chang S. Dietary intake of selected fatty acids, cholesterol and carotenoids and estrogen receptor status in premenopausal breast cancer patients. *Breast Cancer Res Treat.* 2002;75(1):5–14.

Meterissian S, Kontogiannea M, Murty H, Gupta A. Omega-6 fatty acids can inhibit fas-mediated apoptosis in a human colorectal carcinoma cell line: A potential mechanism for escape from immune surveillance. *Int J Surg Investig.* 2000;2(4):253–257.

Mitchell HG, Wei-Cheng Y. A factorial trial including garlic supplements assesses effect in reducing precancerous gastric lesions: Significance of garlic and its constituents in cancer and cardiovascular disease. *J Nutr.* 2006;136:813S–815S.

Ravasco P, Monteiro-Grillo I, Vidal PM, Camilo ME. Dietary counseling improves patient outcomes: A prospective, randomized, controlled trial in colorectal cancer patients undergoing radiotherapy. *J Clin Oncol.* 2005;23(7):1431–1438.

Rose P, Huang Q, Ong CN, Whiteman M. Broccoli and watercress suppress matrix metalloproteinase-9 activity and invasiveness of human MDA-MB-231 breast cancer cells. *Toxicol Appl Pharmacol.* 2005;209(2): 105–113.

Sharp GB, Lagarde F, Mizuno T, et al. Relationship of hepatocellular carcinoma to soya food consumption: A cohort-based, case-control study in Japan. *Int J Cancer.* 2005;115(2):290–295.

Skaper SD, et al. Quercetin protects cutaneous tissue-associated cell types including sensory neurons from oxidative stress induced by glutathione depletion: Cooperative effects of ascorbic acid. *Free Radic Biol Med.* 1997;22(4):669–678.

Srivastava AR, Dalela D. Prostate cancer: Altering the natural history by dietary changes. *Natl Med J India.* 2004; 17(5):248–253.

Tang L, Li G, Song L, Zhang Y. The principal urinary metabolites of dietary isothiocyanates, N-acetylcysteine conjugates, elicit the same anti-proliferative response as their parent compounds in human bladder cancer cells. *Anticancer Drugs.* 2006;17(3):297–305.

van der Hulst RR, van Kreel BK, von Meyenfeldt MF, et al. Glutamine and the preservation of gut integrity. *Lancet.* 1993;341:1363–1365.

Wood JD, Enser M, Fisher AV, Nute GR, Richardson RI, Sheard PR. Manipulating meat quality and composition. *Proc Nutr Soc.* 1999;58(2):363–370.

INDEX